Making CONNECTIONS 2

Skills and Strategies for Academic Reading

Second Edition

Teacher's Manual

Jo McEntire | Jessica Williams

CAMBRIDGE
UNIVERSITY PRESS

CAMBRIDGE
UNIVERSITY PRESS

32 Avenue of the Americas, New York, NY 10013-2473, USA

Cambridge University Press is part of the University of Cambridge.

It furthers the University's mission by disseminating knowledge in the pursuit of education, learning and research at the highest international levels of excellence.

www.cambridge.org
Information on this title: www.cambridge.org/9781107650626

First published 2008
Second edition 2013
3rd printing 2014

Printed in the United States of America

A catalog record for this publication is available from the British Library.

ISBN 978-1-107-62874-8 Student's Book
ISBN 978-1-107-65062-6 Teacher's Manual

Layout services and book design: Page Designs International, Inc.
Cover design: Studio Montage

Contents

Teaching Suggestions

The *Making Connections 2* Student's Book consists of six units, each of which is organized in the following way:

- Two Skills and Strategies sections alternate with the readings. The first precedes Readings 1 and 2, and the second precedes Readings 3 and 4. These sections introduce and practice specific skills and strategies for reading.
- Four readings are each accompanied by associated activities in reading and vocabulary development. The fourth reading is the longest and offers students a reading experience similar to the challenges of the reading assignments they will meet in their future academic studies.
- A final section, Making Connections, provides two cohesion-building exercises.

Intermediate-level students need to expand their vocabulary in order to prepare for academic courses. Strategies and activities to help students expand their vocabulary are therefore important features of *Making Connections 2*. The post-reading activities following each of the four readings in a unit include tasks that facilitate vocabulary expansion by focusing on 18–20 vocabulary items used in the reading. Additionally, tasks for vocabulary from the Academic Word List (AWL) follow the second and fourth readings. All vocabulary items are listed and defined, with an example provided, in Appendix 1 of the Student's Book (pages 257–268). In Appendix 2 of the Student's Book (pages 269–270), each key vocabulary item is indexed by the unit and the reading in which it is first used. The icon indicates vocabulary items from the AWL.

Making Connections 2 has enough material for a reading course of 50 to 70 class hours, assuming a corresponding number of hours are available for homework assignments. Completing all the Beyond the Reading activities that accompany each reading might make the course longer.

Skills, strategies, and vocabulary are recycled within a unit and in subsequent units. It is recommended, therefore, that in planning a course outline, the order of the book be followed.

Skills and Strategies

The Skills and Strategies sections introduce reading and vocabulary-building strategies that are then incorporated into the reading activities.

Rationale

Research suggests that good readers apply various strategies when they are reading a text. The Skills and Strategies sections introduce and provide practice with a variety of these reading strategies.

Description

The first Skills and Strategies section of each unit introduces vocabulary-building skills and strategies: understanding vocabulary in context, using the dictionary, the vocabulary of numbers, vocabulary study, and collocation. The second Skills and Strategies section in each unit focuses on reading strategies: finding main ideas and supporting details, understanding information in graphs and charts, scanning, taking notes, and preparing for a reading test.

Each Skills and Strategies section provides two to three Skill Practice activities that move students from recognition to production. More practice is provided in the While You Read section. Students then review each skill and strategy within the Skill Review section. Strategies are recycled throughout the text.

How to Use

The Skills and Strategies sections are best introduced in class, supported by the use of other materials (e.g., examples similar to those in the Examples & Explanations subsection). At the beginning of the course, each of the Skill Practice activities should be partially completed in class. Then, when you are confident that your students understand the form and content of each activity, an appropriate number of items can be assigned for homework.

Before You Read

Connecting to the Topic

Rationale

The purpose of this activity is to get students to activate background knowledge relevant to the content of the reading that follows. Effective reading occurs when readers are able to place new information within the context of information they already possess.

Description

This is the first of two activities that occur before each reading. It consists of questions for discussion with a partner.

How to Use

This activity can be introduced through short, full-class discussions. Partners or small groups can then continue the discussions.

Previewing and Predicting

Rationale

The purpose of this activity is to get students into the habit of previewing the content and organization of a text before they start reading in depth. Previewing has been shown to be a key strategy that enhances a reader's ability to understand a text on first encounter.

Description

Making Connections 2 uses different techniques for previewing texts. Students are taught to look at titles, headings, pictures, and graphic information such as charts to guess what information might appear, or to form questions that they expect a reading to answer. Each technique encourages the student to interact with the text before beginning to read for deeper understanding.

How to Use

These activities are best introduced, modeled, and practiced in class. We recommend that students first work with a partner. The primary goal of this activity is to encourage active interaction with the text.

While You Read

Rationale

Research suggests that good readers read actively by asking themselves questions and monitoring comprehension as they read. The While You Read tasks encourage students to adopt this approach. These tasks focus students' attention on the strategic nature of the reading process during their first read-through of a text. These tasks appear in the margins of the text and force students to stop and apply the strategies presented in the earlier Skills and Strategies sections. Students are thus encouraged to do what good readers do – to interact with the text while they read.

Description

While You Read boxes are in the margin of every reading, opposite some words in bold blue within a line of text. Students are directed to stop reading at the end of the sentence containing the bold blue text and to perform a strategic task designed to support effective reading.

While You Read provides practice for the skills and strategies previously introduced. It reinforces lexical skills by having students identify context clues to meaning, figure out a word's part of speech, look up challenging words in a dictionary, and recognize collocations. It provides practice in reading skills by having students identify main ideas and supporting details and understand connections between paragraphs.

How to Use

While You Read is best introduced and modeled as a classroom activity after the reading has been previewed. We recommend that you first introduce students to the concept of active reading. You can do this by reading the first reading of Unit 1 out loud. As you come to each bold blue word, stop and read the While You Read directions. Answer the question before you continue to read. Note that this technique will be new to many students, particularly those who do not read extensively in their own language. Students will find it a time-consuming process at first, but assure them that, with practice, they will gradually apply these strategies automatically and their reading speed and comprehension will increase.

At first, many of the boxes in the shorter readings can be completed during an initial in-class read-through. This will allow you to provide students with the intensive guidance, practice, and immediate feedback on their performances that they will need as they learn to apply these skills independently.

To help students focus on the reading process, it is strongly recommended that no dictionary be used during this first read-through. We also recommend that the first read-through include reading for main ideas. (See the Main Idea Check section below.)

One challenge in the While You Read activity is that students tend to make excessive use of highlighting and/or underlining. Try to help students understand that highlighting or underlining entire paragraphs, for example, is not an effective reading strategy. In fact, indiscriminate highlighting is a counterproductive activity. To avoid this, have the students follow the directions provided in the Skills and Strategies sections: highlight main ideas only, number supporting details, and underline key vocabulary.

Reading Skill Development

Main Idea Check

Rationale

Students often focus too much on the details in a reading rather than on its main ideas. The Main Idea Check activity provides an opportunity for students to focus on an understanding of the main ideas of each paragraph. It is only after students have grasped the main ideas of a reading that they can make sense of how the details fit into this larger frame of meaning.

Description

For the first two readings of Unit 1, the Main Idea Check asks students to choose from four options the sentence that best expresses the main idea of the entire reading. For the remainder of the readings, the Main Idea Check has students identify the main idea of different paragraphs by matching the paragraph number to the sentence expressing its main idea.

How to Use

Before starting the Main Idea Check tasks in Unit 1, we recommend that you read Skills and Strategies 2 in Unit 1 so that you know the main idea identification strategies that will be explicitly introduced there.

For Unit 1, Readings 1 and 2, use a simple approach with which you are comfortable, without going into the issue in any great detail. It would be helpful, for example, to have students discuss why the other choices do not represent the main idea of the reading.

After you work through the strategy-based approach to main idea identification in Skills and Strategies 2, Unit 1, the Main Idea Check tasks may be assigned for work in class or for homework. In classes with additional writing goals, students could be asked to rewrite the sentences of the Main Idea Check tasks in their own words and then put the sentences together to form a summary of the given reading.

A Closer Look

Rationale

Having understood the main ideas in a reading, students need to achieve a more in-depth understanding of it. In this activity, therefore, students are asked to go back to the reading and read for details and to establish connections among them.

Description

Many of the questions in A Closer Look are types of questions with which students will probably be familiar (e.g., true/false and multiple choice). We recommend that early on in the text, perhaps in Unit 2, you review some common strategies in answering multiple-choice questions. You can encourage students to use the following strategies:

- Read the directions very carefully.
- Read all the possible answers before choosing the correct one.
- Eliminate the obviously incorrect answers.
- Recognize that a wrong answer may include an incorrect fact or information not in the reading.
- Recognize that all information within the answer must be true for the answer to be correct.

You should also alert students to one question type that is possibly less familiar. To encourage the synthesizing of information, a significant number of multiple-choice questions have more than one correct answer. This question type is introduced by the directions *Circle all that apply*.

How to Use

Generally, the tasks in A Closer Look lend themselves well to completion outside of class. However, we suggest that at first you give students some classroom practice in answering this section.

A useful tool for students as they complete A Closer Look tasks is Appendix 1, Key Vocabulary (pages 257–268 in the Student's Book). This appendix lists the vocabulary alphabetically within each reading, thus providing accessible and convenient support for students during these more detailed examinations of the readings. For more information on Appendix 1, see page 7 of this Teacher's Manual.

Skill Review

Rationale

Students need multiple opportunities to practice new reading and vocabulary-building skills and strategies. This is particularly important as new skills are introduced that build upon understanding of those previously taught.

Description

The Skill Review allows students to practice specific skills introduced in the Skills and Strategies sections. The content reflects the previous reading, and therefore should be sufficiently familiar to enable students to focus on the skill itself.

How to Use

This is a good homework assignment. Students can then compare their work in small groups. If students encounter problems with this task, direct them back to the appropriate Skills and Strategies section. It is worth taking the time in class to really explain these tasks since they are key to academic reading.

Vocabulary Development

Definitions

Rationale

This activity provides a simple and structured way for students to take their first steps in learning the target vocabulary in each of the 24 readings.

Description

In this activity, students find a word in the reading that is similar in meaning to each of 10 given definitions. This is a simple way for students to focus on target vocabulary in context without having to use bilingual dictionaries. Part-of-speech information about the target vocabulary has been provided so that students can integrate this information into the vocabulary-learning process.

How to Use

This activity is best introduced as a classroom activity. It can then be completed either in or out of class as homework.

Words in Context

Rationale

Understanding the meaning of unknown target words by perceiving the surrounding context of the word has been demonstrated to be an important skill in vocabulary acquisition. This activity helps students to see the linguistic contexts in which the target words belong.

Description

There are three types of Words in Context activities: fill-in-the-blank within sentences, fill-in-the blanks within paragraphs, and matching. All activities introduce words or phrases from the readings that have not been targeted in the preceding Definitions exercise. The key vocabulary items are presented at the beginning of the activity.

How to Use

This activity can be completed either in or out of class. Encourage students to go back to the reading and find the target words if they cannot readily answer the questions. Although these words are recycled in later readings, we encourage you to expand this practice by creating vocabulary tests focusing on these target words. Testing students on some of the vocabulary from Unit 1 while they are working on later units, for example, will help them to retain vocabulary.

Synonyms

Rationale

Students need multiple ways to learn key vocabulary. The Synonyms activity offers the chance to focus on the meaning of key words by connecting that meaning to familiar words and phrases.

Description

Each item in the activity requires students to select the correct target vocabulary word or phrase that is closest in meaning to the words in parentheses. Students then use this information to fill in the blank lines for each sentence.

How to Use

This activity is appropriate for both in and out of class work.

Word Families

Rationale

Intermediate-level learners need to build their academic vocabulary quickly in order to be successful in more advanced courses. Recognizing different word forms allows students to increase their receptive vocabulary quickly and efficiently. By focusing on parts of speech, this approach to vocabulary building also may help students move toward the ability to use the vocabulary in writing and speech.

Description

This activity is introduced after the second reading of each unit. It introduces five word families. The boldface word in each family is the part of speech that appears in the reading. Students are instructed to locate the words in the reading and use context clues to figure out the meanings. If the students are still unsure, you may direct them to Appendix 1 on pages 257–268 to check the meaning of unfamiliar vocabulary. Students choose the correct word form to complete the 10 fill-in-the-blank sentences.

How to Use

We recommend that you introduce this activity in class, as students may need more instruction in parts of speech. They may also need guidance in using the correct form of the word.

Academic Word List

Rationale

The *Academic Word List* (Coxhead, 2000) provides a corpus of the most frequently used academic words. *Making Connections 2* provides students with the opportunity to learn this vocabulary, an activity that is key to preparing for academic coursework in all fields of study.

Description

Situated after the second and fourth readings, this fill-in-the-sentence activity focuses on AWL vocabulary items from the two preceding readings.

How to Use

Before you begin this activity, it is important to explain the significance of general academic vocabulary. Make sure that students know AWL items are not technical, subject-specific terms but rather general words common to all academic coursework. Research has shown that students need familiarity with this vocabulary in order to understand college texts.

The Academic Word List activity provides an opportunity for students to go back to the readings and explore vocabulary if needed. This can be done out of class, but it also works well as a group activity with students discussing possible answers and referring to the readings to explain their choices. It is recommended that students learn this vocabulary by making word cards.

Beyond the Reading

Critical Thinking

Rationale

A successful college student does not merely accumulate information. Rather, that student engages in thoughtful, reflective, and independent thinking in order to make sense of a text. Critical thinking skills enable a student to evaluate what they read, make connections, ask questions, solve problems, and apply that information to new situations.

Description

Each Critical Thinking activity defines a specific critical thinking skill and then allows students to practice that skill in a context linked to the previous reading. Examples of specific skills include clarifying concepts, applying information to new situations, and offering opinions.

How to Use

Before you begin this activity, it is a good idea to discuss the difference between memorization and comprehension. Introduce critical thinking skills as an essential part of comprehension. This is particularly important as some students may come from educational systems that emphasize rote learning rather than critical thinking. The activity itself could be assigned to in-class groups or as homework. The latter would allow students to spend time exploring the specific critical thinking skill. Students could then compare their responses in groups.

Research

Rationale

Some teachers may want to use the readings as an opportunity for their students to undertake some research on the topics of the readings.

Description

This activity occurs after each of the 24 readings. It offers topics for students to research and discuss that are relevant to the subject of a reading.

How to Use

The research questions offer opportunities for students to tackle more challenging reading tasks as well as to pursue more personally stimulating aspects of a given topic. Some of the research requires students to do self-reflection or survey classmates to gather more data. Some require students to go online to find additional information.

Writing

Rationale

Students develop deeper understanding of a reading and become more adept at using new vocabulary if provided an opportunity to reflect and write about what they have read.

Description

This writing activity appears at the close of each reading. It allows students to use their discussion and research activity as the basis to write two short paragraphs.

How to Use

The paragraphs can be produced in or outside of class. Remind students to use information from their research activity within their writing. It is also a good idea to encourage them to use new vocabulary they have learned from that unit.

Improving Your Reading Speed

Rationale

Slow reading is a common complaint of second-language learners. It is frustrating, and it impedes comprehension. While individuals will read at different rates, gradually increasing rates for all students will allow students to read more effectively and with more pleasure and confidence.

Description

This activity appears at the end of each second and fourth reading. Students are directed to choose one of the previous readings within the unit and time themselves as they read. They then record their time in a chart in Appendix 3 on pages 272–273. This practice provides the opportunity for students to see their reading speed improve as they practice.

How to Use

We do not recommend that teachers suggest an ideal words-per-minute reading rate for two reasons. First, students will read at different rates. Equally important, good readers vary their rate according to a text and reading purpose. Instead, focus on improving individual rates while stressing that effective reading involves both adequate speed and comprehension.

Have students read Appendix 3 before they complete this activity. This will allow the students to learn and practice strategies that will improve their reading rates. It is also important that students identify personal reading habits, such as reading out loud or looking at each individual word, that slow down reading rates.

It is a good idea to complete this activity in class the first time. You might need to help students compute their words-per-minute rates and enter these in their charts. Most of all, stress that like any skill, improving reading speed requires practice.

Making Connections

As the final review activity of each unit, two exercises give students practice in establishing within short texts the cohesion of vocabulary, structural features, and organizational patterns.

Rationale

These tasks provide students with a focused opportunity to practice reading for cohesion between sentences and short paragraphs. In addition, students get a further opportunity to review recently targeted academic vocabulary.

Description

Units 1 to 4 introduce and give students practice with strategies writers use to achieve cohesion:

- Repetition of key words or phrases
- Use of pronoun and antecedent connectors

- Use of cause-and-effect transition connectors
- Use of contrast transition words

Units 5 and 6 allow students to review and apply all four strategies. Practice begins at the sentence level and progresses to short paragraphs. Target vocabulary from the unit is recycled throughout this Making Connections section.

How to Use

This section is probably best performed in class, where fairly immediate feedback is available. Students can work individually or in pairs. Feedback may be supplied by you and/or elicited from students. You can expand this practice by presenting other jigsaw-type activities. For example, use a paragraph that has the same cohesion-building strategies.

Appendices

Appendix 1: Key Vocabulary
(Pages 257–268)

Appendix 1 is the "dictionary" for *Making Connections 2*. For each reading, the target vocabulary items are listed alphabetically, defined simply and clearly, and exemplified in a sentence. The dictionary's purpose

is to offer students easy access to information on the meaning and use of each word during the vocabulary learning process, especially while they are completing the Vocabulary Development activities. It can also be used during students' work on A Closer Look. Note that vocabulary from the AWL is indicated by the icon.

Appendix 2: Index To Key Vocabulary
(Pages 269–270)

Appendix 2 is an index that lists each key vocabulary item by the unit and the reading in which it is first introduced, thus allowing students to locate the original dictionary entry for a vocabulary item when necessary.

Note that vocabulary from the AWL is indicated by the icon.

Appendix 3: Improving Your Reading Speed (Pages 271–273)

Appendix 3 begins with a list of strategies students can employ in order to improve their reading speed. It is a good idea to discuss these strategies before students practice this skill. It also includes a chart that students will use to record their reading rates as they work through the Student's Book.

Answer Key

1 The News Media

Skills and Strategies 1
Understanding Vocabulary In Context

Skill Practice 1 *Page 3*

2. b For instance
3. c In contrast
4. b such as
5. a They weren't exactly sure of the number because there were too many people to count.
6. a . . . , those who cannot read or write,

Skill Practice 2 *Page 4*

2. b	5. c
3. c	6. a
4. b	

Skill Practice 3 *Page 5*

2. different from the usual
3. providing a lot of useful information
4. people who buy things
5. very shocking
6. stop from doing something you want to do
7. good; hopeful and confident

Reading 1
The News Media in the Past

Connecting to the Topic *Page 6*
Answers will vary.

Previewing and Predicting *Page 6*
a

While You Read

1. asked travelers; gather around and listen.
2. could not read
3. large wires

Reading Skill Development

Main Idea Check *Page 9*
a

A Closer Look *Page 9*

1. False
2. d
3. c
4. a, d
5. False
6. 1690   The first U.S. newspaper started in Boston.
   1752   The first newspaper in Canada started.
   1840s Newspapers became cheaper and more popular.
   1860s Telegraph cables under the oceans were introduced.
   1883   Krakatoa erupted.

Skill Review *Page 10*
A

WORD OR PHRASE	DEFINI-TION	EXEMPLI-FICATION	CONTRAST	GENERAL KNOW-LEDGE
prior to (adv) Par. 1	✓			
invention (n) Par. 3		✓		
brief (adj) Par. 3		✓		
spanned (v) Par. 5		✓		
functioning (v) Par. 5			✓	

B

1. c	4. b
2. a	5. a
3. c	

Vocabulary Development

Definitions *Page 11*

1. local	6. afford
2. villagers	7. immigrants
3. gather	8. eager
4. crimes	9. wires
5. terrified	10. volcano

Words in Context *Page 11*

1. focused on
2. natural disasters
3. publish
4. erupt
5. average
6. assassinated
7. appetite
8. dramatically

Reading 2
The History of Electronic Media

Connecting to the Topic *Page 13*

Answers will vary.

Previewing and Predicting *Page 13*

PARAGRAPH	QUESTION
3	How did early television change the news?
2	What changes made the radio more convenient?
1	What was the next development in the news after newspapers?
5	What are the newest changes in the media?
4	How has television news changed the world?

While You Read

1. at the same time that they were happening
2. Even poor people or people who lived far away from any city could now easily listen to a radio.
3. 24 hours a day; 7 days a week
4. smart phones; MP3 players

Reading Skill Development

Main Idea Check *Page 16*

d

A Closer Look *Page 16*

1. a, c, d
2. True
3. c
4. b
5. False
6.

TRADITIONAL	DIGITAL
Newspapers	computers
Television	smart phones
	MP3 players
	tablets

Skill Review *Page 17*

A

1. b
2. f
3. d
4. a
5. e
6. c

B

1. sole
2. far-reaching
3. bulky
4. forced
5. views
6. Revolution

Vocabulary Development

Definitions *Page 18*

1. transmit
2. live
3. Convenient
4. batteries
5. negative
6. broadcasting
7. Global
8. impact
9. available
10. Pace

Word Families *Page 18*

1. access
2. influential
3. traditions
4. acceleration
5. traditional
6. influence
7. significant
8. access
9. accelerate
10. significance

Academic Word List *Page 19*

1. negative
2. impact
3. accessible
4. dramatically
5. global
6. traditional
7. focuses on
8. publish
9. transmitted
10. access to

Skills and Strategies 2
Finding Main Ideas

Skill Practice 1 *Page 22*

1. a
2. b
3. a
4. d

Skill Practice 2 *Page 23*

1. d
2. c
3. b
4. c

Skill Practice 3 *Page 24*

1. c
2. d
3. Pulitzer wanted journalism to be a respected profession.

Reading 3
Citizen Journalism

Connecting to the Topic *Page 25*

Answers will vary.

Previewing and Predicting *Page 25*

PARAGRAPH	TOPIC
2	It will explain how news was reported in the past before citizen journalism
4	It will give a detailed example of one online news site.
1	It will describe changes in the news media today.
7	It will describe recent changes in the news business.
6	It will describe problems of citizen journalism.
5	It will explain how traditional journalists and citizen journalists can work together.
3	It will explain how traditional journalists are losing control over the news.

While You Read

1. citizen journalists
2. reporters and editors decided what news to publish and what news to ignore
3. adding, or posting, comments to the blog
4. the power of citizen journalism

Reading Skill Development

Main Idea Check *Page 28*

A 2   D 7
B 4   E 6
C 3   F 5

A Closer Look *Page 28*

1. False   5. b
2. d   6. a, c, d, e
3. True   7. True
4. d   8. a

Skill Review *Page 29*

PARA-GRAPH NUMBER	FIRST SEN-TENCE	SECOND SEN-TENCE	LAST SEN-TENCE	WHOLE PARA-GRAPH
2	✓			
3		✓		
4				✓
5	✓			
6	✓			
7	✓			

Vocabulary Development

Definitions *Page 30*

1. transform   6. devastation
2. research   7. Survivors
3. editors   8. attack
4. worthwhile   9. last
5. ignore   10. solution

Words in Context *Page 30*

1. f   5. b
2. h   6. g
3. a   7. c
4. e   8. d

Reading 4
Ethical Reporting

Connecting to the Topic *Page 32*

Answers will vary.

Previewing and Predicting *Page 32*

c

While You Read

1. they don't tell people they are reporters. They pretend to be someone else so they can go to places where reporters cannot usually go.
2. illegal activities
3. journalists must always tell the truth
4. a) First sentence
5. reporters also take photographs of the rich and famous

Reading Skill Development

Main Idea Check *Page 36*

A 3
B 4
C 9
D 6
E 10

A Closer Look *Page 36*

1. b, d
2. a
3. True
4. True
5. 4, 5, 1, 3, 6, 2
6. True
7. b
8. 1 d, 2 a, 3 e, 4 c, 5 b

Skill Review *Page 37*

PARAGRAPH	CLAIM 1	CLAIM 2
7	✓	
8		✓
9		✓
10	✓	

Vocabulary Development

Definitions *Page 38*

1. pressure
2. pretend
3. mentally ill
4. Security
5. fake
6. documents
7. illegal
8. shocked
9. addict
10. celebrities

Words in Context *Page 38*

1. a sensational
   b poisonous
   c confessed
   d resigned
2. e privacy
   f complained
   g benefit
   h arrested

Academic Word List *Page 39*

1. security
2. documents
3. illegal
4. survivors
5. benefits
6. research
7. rejected
8. concept
9. ignore
10. transformed

Making Connections

Exercise 1 *Page 41*

2. July 20th, 1969 – *That day*
   watched – *watched*
   people all over the world – *international television audience*
3. bureaus – *these news bureaus*
   international – *all over the world*
   smaller newspapers – *smaller companies*

Exercise 2 *Page 42*

1. CAB
2. BAC
3. CAB
4. CBA
5. BAC

2 Education

Skills and Strategies 3
Using the Dictionary

Skill Practice 1 *Page 45*

1. b   4. a
2. b   5. b
3. a

Skill Practice 2 *Page 46*

1. b   4. b
2. b   5. a
3. a

Skill Practice 3 *Page 47*

2. find a similarity or connection between things
3. left someone or something in a difficult situation
4. right or just
5. doing the same thing at the same time and/or the same place
6. changed
7. learn something completely
8. very important
9. very sure
10. not strong

Reading 1
Education Around the World

Connecting to the Topic *Page 48*
Answers will vary.

Previewing and Predicting *Page 48*
Answers will vary.

While You Read

1. When industrialization began
2. b) the first and second
3. although
4. b) Easy to understand

Reading Skill Development

Main Idea Check *Page 51*

A 2   D 1
B 3   E 6
C 4   F 5

A Closer Look *Page 51*

1. c   4. True
2. a   5. b
3. c   6. c

Skill Review *Page 52*

1. a. (*n*): *a particular position, degree, or amount*
   b. Answers will vary.
2. a. (*v*): *to be successful in a test, exam, or course*
   b. Answers will vary.
3. a. (*n*): *an occasion that allows something to be done; an opportunity*
   b. Answers will vary.
4. a. (*n*): *a space or position in a line of people waiting to do something*
   b. Answers will vary.

Vocabulary Development

Definitions *Page 53*

1. expand   6. opportunity
2. Development   7. elsewhere
3. compulsory   8. curriculum
4. scores   9. vary
5. emphasize   10. productivity

Words in Context *Page 53*

1. industrialization   5. funding
2. individuals   6. advantage
3. meet the need   7. academic
4. contributes to   8. fees

Reading 2
Testing in Education

Connecting to the Topic *Page 55*
Answers will vary.

Previewing and Predicting *Page 55*

PARAGRAPH	TOPIC
3	Tests after secondary school
6	How tests can affect health
4	Test pressure in university exams
5	Test preparation programs
7	Tests of national performance
2	The impact of test results on a student's future

While You Read

1. The score on these standardized tests can often determine a student's educational future.
2. a) examples: India, Tanzania, and Malaysia
3. a) Noun
4. students had seen the exam questions before the day of the exam
5. Nations also use tests to evaluate educational performance.

Reading Skill Development

Main Idea Check *Page 59*

A 4   D 5
B 3   E 2
C 7   F 6

A Closer Look *Page 59*

1. False   5. c
2. b, c   6. a, b
3. b, d   7. b, c
4. True

Skill Review *Page 60*

PARA-GRAPH NUMBER	FIRST SEN-TENCE	SECOND SEN-TENCE	LAST SEN-TENCE	WHOLE PARA-GRAPH
2				✓
3		✓		
4				✓
5	✓			
6		✓		
7		✓		

Vocabulary Development

Definitions *Page 61*

1. measure   6. Cheating
2. colonies   7. obtain
3. Factors   8. profitable
4. consider   9. compare
5. enormous   10. policy

Word Families *Page 61*

1. competition   6. evaluated
2. performance   7. perform
3. evaluation   8. argue
4. argument   9. efficient
5. efficiency   10. competed

Academic Word List *Page 62*

1. academic   6. factor
2. emphasize   7. obtained
3. policy   8. enormous
4. individual   9. evaluated
5. contribute to   10. expand

Skills and Strategies 4
Finding Supporting Details

Skill Practice 1 *Page 65*

1. A-S, B-M   3. A-M, B-S
2. A-M, B-S   4. A-S, B-M

Skill Practice 2 *Page 66*

1. A-S, B-M, C-S   3. A-S, B-S, C-M
2. A-S, B-M, C-S   4. A-S, B-S, C-M

Skill Practice 3 *Page 66*

1. The teacher had no training.
   She was sometimes only 16.
   She had to sweep and cook.
   She had to teach all subjects to all ages.
2. Immigrants have always had to learn English.
   Speaking English all the time is the best way to learn.
   It will be harder for children if they speak two languages.
3. The teacher gave them new names.
   They cut their hair.
   They were only permitted to speak English.
   They were not allowed to practice their own religion.

Reading 3
Alternative Education

Connecting to the Topic Page 68

Answers will vary.

Previewing and Predicting Page 68

A, C, E, G, H

While You Read

1. designed in the 1950s, and that they have not changed to fit the needs of today's workplace
2. a) (*n*) A need or desire
3. disagree with standardized tests; do not like a traditional curriculum; emphasize religious instruction; an opportunity to spend more time with their children; they can do a better job of teaching their children
4. The fastest growing form of alternative education is *distance learning* – taking classes online.
5. Some students may complete a course quickly; others may take much longer.

Reading Skill Development

Main Idea Check Page 72

A 8	D 7
B 2	E 9
C 4	

A Closer Look Page 72

1. a	5. b
2. b, c	6. b
3. True	7. True
4. False	8. a, d

Skill Review Page 73
A

1. 1	4. 1
2. 2	5. 2
3. 1	6. 2

B

1. Others choose to homeschool because they want to emphasize religious instruction, . . . (Par. 4)
2. Learners can study when they want to. They do no not need to attend classes at a particular time. (Par. 7)
3. Parents may also see homeschooling as an opportunity to spend more time with their children. (Par. 4)
4. . . . some do not like a traditional curriculum (Par. 4)
5. Many online courses also allow students to work at their own pace. (Par. 7)
6. Location is one important factor. Distance learners can live in one city and take classes from another city – or even another country – without ever leaving home. (Par. 6)

Vocabulary Development

Definitions Page 74

1. criticize	6. Statistics
2. concerned	7. Approximate
3. obsolete	8. location
4. Approaches	9. dissatisfied
5. shortage	10. likely

Words in Context Page 74

1. a	hands-on	2. e	high-tech
	b design		f estimate
	c workplace		g especially
	d alternative		h concentrate on

Reading 4
Skills for the Twenty-First Century

Connecting to the Topic Page 76

Answers will vary.

Previewing and Predicting Page 76

SECTION	TOPIC
II	A description of skills people need today
IV	An evaluation of how different countries are teaching twenty-first century skills
V	An explanation of why twenty-first-century skills are essential
III	An explanation about how people use skills while they are working
I	Background information about how the meaning of *literacy* changed through history

While You Read

1. Topic: twenty-first century skills; Claim: they are very different from skills people needed in the past
2. First, they can find information, such as text, videos, and audio files, from different sources; Next, they know how to evaluate these sources to make sure the information is current and accurate; Finally, students use a range of technology tools and software programs to present their information to others.
3. In other words, critical thinkers ask questions about the world around them.
4. b) beginning
5. lend them money
6. this difference in access to technology
7. It is difficult to estimate how well schools are teaching critical thinking.

Reading Skill Development

Main Idea Check *Page 80*

A 6   D 9
B 7   E 2
C 3

A Closer Look *Page 80*

1. b   5. c
2. a   6. d
3. a, b, e   7. True
4. a, c

Skill Review *Page 81*

Para 3
  a Clear communication
  b Collaboration; ability to work in a group
  c Communication across cultures; languages

Para 8
  a Europe + China teach English to primary school students
  b 725,000 international students in U.S.
  c 400,000 in G.B. 475,000 in Australia

Vocabulary Development

Definitions *Page 82*

1. expert   6. launch
2. collaborate   7. Effectively
3. require   8. investors
4. Curiosity   9. lend
5. encourage   10. regions

Synonyms *Page 82*

1. current   5. creative
2. accurate   6. incorporated
3. range   7. encounter
4. analyzed   8. essential

Academic Word List *Page 83*

1. alternative   6. analyze
2. creative   7. encounter
3. incorporated   8. range
4. design   9. expert
5. estimated   10. approximate

Making Connections

Exercise 1 *Page 85*

1. They – *parents*
  they – *parents*
2. This – *fastest growing alternative education is distance learning*
  it – *distance learning*
3. They – *students*
  this – *collaborate on their final project*
  it – *final project*
4. it – *primary education*
  This – *primary education is free*

Exercise 2 *Page 86*

1. BAC   4. CAB
2. ABC   5. BCA
3. BAC

3 The World of Business

Skills and Strategies 5
The Vocabulary of Numbers

Skill Practice 1 *Page 89*

Answers will vary.
1. increased / rose / grew; increase
2. fell / declined / dropped / went down
3. rapidly / significantly / sharply / dramatically
4. grew / increased / rose
5. grew / increased / rose
6. grow / rise / go up / increase

Skill Practice 2 *Page 90*

Answers will vary.
1. The cost of eggs increased from 18 cents per dozen to 71 cents per dozen.
2. The cost fell sharply from 71 cents per dozen to 39 cents per dozen.
3. The cost rose dramatically from 39 cents per dozen to 91 cents per dozen.
4. The cost went up to $1.88 per dozen.
5. I think the cost will continue to rise steadily in the future.

Skill Practice 3 *Page 90*

Answers will vary, but students should include a variety of vocabulary from page 88.

Reading 1
Supply and Demand in the Global Economy

Connecting to the Topic *Page 91*

Answers will vary.

Previewing and Predicting *Page 91*

A, C, D

While You Read

1. rose; increase; increased
2. as prices rise, demand falls
3. businesses; must have enough of a product to sell
4. A change in supply can have a global effect.

Reading Skill Development

Main Idea Check *Page 94*

A 2   D 5
B 6   E 3
C 1   F 4

A Closer Look *Page 94*

1. c   4. B → D → E → A → C
2. c   5. d
3. False

Skill Review *Page 95*

1. b   3. b
2. c   4. d

Vocabulary Development

Definitions *Page 96*

1. illustrate   6. skyrocket
2. plants   7. survive
3. crop   8. ingredient
4. effect   9. protest
5. Approximately   10. major

Words in Context *Page 96*

1. event   5. note
2. surplus   6. previously
3. energy   7. Consumption
4. affects   8. fuel

Reading 2
The Workforce in the Twenty-First Century

Connecting to the Topic *Page 98*

Answers will vary.

Previewing and Predicting *Page 98*

SECTION	QUESTIONS
I	What is a *skilled worker*?
II	What is *outsourcing*?
I	What kind of workers do employers want?
III	What does *mobile* mean?
I	What kinds of jobs require skilled workers?
II	How does outsourcing save money?
III	What is a *global workforce*?

While You Read

1. move parts of the manufacturing process to different countries
2. workers are willing to move away from home to get a good job
3. governments
4. a) First sentence

Reading Skill Development

Main Idea Check *Page 101*

A 2   D 3
B 7   E 6
C 5   F 4

A Closer Look *Page 101*

1. c   4. c
2. d   5. a, c
3. False   6. d

Skill Review *Page 102*

1. This – *when the demand is high and the supply is low, the cost goes up*
2. it – *twenty-first-century workforce*
3. it – *English*
   This – *people all over the world learn it*
4. This – *help the economy of the country that a worker leaves*
   Their – *workers*
5. it – *The total amount of remittances worldwide*

Vocabulary Development

Definitions *Page 103*

1. create   6. blame
2. developing   7. Precisely
3. willing   8. workforce
4. specialists   9. hire
5. practice   10. Challenges

Word Families *Page 103*

1. prevents   6. attract
2. manufactures   7. Manufacturing
3. flexible   8. prevention
4. employ   9. flexibility
5. attractive   10. employment

Academic Word List *Page 104*

1. affects   6. energy
2. challenge   7. previously
3. illustrate   8. precisely
4. approximately   9. major
5. consumption   10. flexible

Skills and Strategies 6
Information in Graphs and Charts

Skill Practice 1 *Page 107*
b

Skill Practice 2 *Page 108*

1. 50,000   6. 350,000
2. 5,000   7. 20,000
3. 100,000   8. 51,000
4. 250,000   9. 620,000
5. 285,000

Skill Practice 3 *Page 109*

1. Green building: does not use much energy and water and does not produce much waste and pollution.
2. Good for business + workers
3. U.S. $71.1 billion
4. U.S. $18.9 billion
5. U.S. $173.5 billion is a 144 percent increase over U.S. $71.1 billion
6. The number of green buildings is increasing, and this helps workers.

Reading 3
Communication Technology in Business

Connecting to the Topic *Page 110*

Answers will vary.

Previewing and Predicting *Page 110*

QUESTION	FIGURE 3.3	FIGURE 3.4
1.	✓	
2.	✓	
3.		✓
4.		✓
5.	✓	
6.		✓

While You Read

1. These tools let people work together more efficiently. They allow them to collect and share different kinds of information in text, pictures, audio, and video, for example.
2. b) Percentage of world's Internet users who live in that country.
3. The motorcycle manufacturing industry in China
4. b) Example
5. new approaches and ideas

Reading Skill Development

Main Idea Check *Page 114*

A 3   D 6
B 4   E 2
C 7   F 5

A Closer Look *Page 114*

1. b, c, e   4. b, c, e
2. a, d   5. b
3. b, d   6. b

Skill Review *Page 115*

1. b   2. a

Vocabulary Development

Definitions *Page 116*

1. share   6. Mining
2. team   7. reward
3. Members   8. Suggestions
4. constant   9. Consumers
5. Interaction   10. promote

Words in Context *Page 116*

1. d   5. b
2. e   6. g
3. a   7. c
4. h   8. f

Reading 4
Business and Sustainability

Connecting to the Topic *Page 118*

Answers will vary.

Previewing and Predicting *Page 118*

SECTION	TOPIC
II	Why consumers want sustainable products
III	Changes to make businesses more sustainable
II	Fossil fuels and air pollution
II	Sustainable products
I	Human damage to the environment
II	The solar power business

While You Read

1. using up natural resources; polluting air and water; climate change
2. it pollutes the air; it uses oil; cars also emit carbon dioxide (CO_2) into the air
3. grown; increase; grew by; increase
4. a type of wood that grows very quickly and is a more renewable resource than other tropical woods.
5. reusing old materials in new ways
6. Save money; improve image

Reading Skill Development

Main Idea Check *Page 122*

A 4   D 7
B 9   E 3
C 2

A Closer Look *Page 122*

1. c   4. False
2. a, b, d   5. d
3. D → C → B → A   6. b

Skill Review *Page 123*

1. 1950
2. increase in cars
3. They will continue to increase.
4. sales of solar energy panels, cost of solar energy panels
5. 2009
6. The cost began to decrease so more people wanted to buy it. As a result, production increased.

Vocabulary Development

Definitions *Page 124*

1. use up
2. Resources
3. Climate
4. Droughts
5. eventually
6. run out
7. renewable
8. hybrid
9. Primarily
10. image

Words in Context *Page 124*

1. a tropical
   b level
   c floods
   d damage
2. e solar
   f reduce
   g emit
   h pollute

Academic Word List *Page 125*

1. constant
2. interaction
3. innovation
4. distributed
5. promote
6. teams
7. participation
8. image
9. role
10. consumers

Making Connections

Exercise 1 *Page 127*

2. Rising oil prices can *C* cause changes *E* in the price of other energy sources. Corn is an alternative source of energy. As oil prices *C* rise, some businesses may start to produce *E* ethanol, a fuel made from corn. As a result of growing *C* demand, corn prices *E* may increase dramatically.

3. A decline in the economy can be good for education. When the economy is good, there are lots *C* of jobs that pay well. As a result, students leave school *E* to find jobs. When the economy declines, there are *C* fewer jobs, so students stay in school. *E*

4. In today's economy, jobs can often move around the world. Global businesses want to keep their labor *C* costs low. So they may move their factories to another *E* country if the labor there is cheaper. This practice is *C* called *outsourcing* and can result in unemployment in *E* the countries with higher labor costs.

Exercise 2 *Page 128*

1. ACB
2. BCA
3. CBA
4. BAC
5. BAC

Population Change and Its Impact

Skills and Strategies 7
Collocations

Skill Practice 1 *Page 131*

Last month business leaders had a meeting at city hall to discuss health and safety in the workplace. There are many immigrants in the city's factories, and leaders are concerned about the workers' language ability. If workers cannot read safety instructions, there could be an accident. The leaders decided on this policy to make sure that their employees stay safe and healthy: (1) Factory managers will read instructions to the employees. (2) If the workers cannot understand the instructions, the managers will find someone who speaks their language to explain the instructions to them. (3) All factory workers must wear safety glasses.

Skill Practice 2 *Page 132*

The population of the world has grown significantly in the second half of the twentieth century. Although the world population did not grow as fast as in the first half of the century, the Earth's population doubled from three billion to six billion people between 1960 and 1999. People were healthier and lived longer than at any time in human history. However, during the same period, changes in the global environment began to accelerate: there was a sharp increase in pollution levels and a continuous decline in natural resources. There is now widespread concern about climate change, and there is strong support for the conclusion that the sea level is rising. What will happen if this population increase continues?

Skill Practice 3 *Page 132*

1. careful attention
2. economic condition
3. healthy food
4. strong evidence
5. low rates
6. steady decline
7. significant difference
8. ethnic groups

Reading 1
Population Trends

Connecting to the Topic *Page 133*

Answers will vary.

Previewing and Predicting *Page 133*

	DEVELOPED WORLD	DEVELOPING WORLD
Population of 1.6 billion in 2000	✓	
More than 2.2 births per woman in 2008		✓
Fewer than 2.2 births per woman in 2008	✓	
Predicted to be more than 7 billion in 2050		✓
Predicted to increase by more than 2 billion between 2000 and 2010		✓
Population of more than 5 billion in 2010		✓

While You Read

1. age range; population trends; world population
2. One of the most important factors is life expectancy. Another important factor is a nation's fertility rate.
3. The fertility rate is the average number of children per woman.
4. Like life expectancy, a country's fertility rate is also related to its development.
5. many countries became concerned about their skyrocketing populations

Reading Skill Development

Main Idea Check *Page 137*

A 5
B 2
C 7
D 4
E 3
F 6

A Closer Look *Page 137*

1. b
2. b
3. d
4. False
5. b
6. a, c, e

Skill Review *Page 138*

1. government programs
2. education level
3. age range
4. population growth
5. fertility rate

Vocabulary Development

Definitions *Page 139*

1. Demography
2. population
3. Trends
4. Figures
5. support
6. Financial
7. Penalties
8. explosion
9. replace
10. retired

Words in Context *Page 139*

1. single
2. take, seriously
3. specific
4. agriculture
5. According to
6. restricts
7. hygiene
8. existing

Reading 2
Global Migration

Connecting to the Topic *Page 141*

Answers will vary.

Previewing and Predicting *Page 141*

PARAGRAPH	QUESTION
3	Where do immigrants typically go when they leave their countries?
6	Is migration good for the countries that migrants leave?
7	Are there negative effects of global migration?
4	Do immigrants always move to countries richer than their home countries?
2	What kind of people are migrants?
5	What effects does global migration have on host countries?

While You Read

1. move from one country to another
2. people who move their homes from one place to another
3. almost as many people move from very poor countries to other countries that are not rich
4. positive impact
5. They can also allow skilled workers in the host country to be more productive

Reading Skill Development

Main Idea Check *Page 144*

A 4   D 7
B 5   E 6
C 3

A Closer Look *Page 144*

1. 2, 3, 1
2. b
3. c
4. a, c, d
5. True
6.

HL / HC	P / N	
HL	P	Money is sent back to migrants' homelands.
HL	N	There are fewer people left to work in the homelands.
HC	P	Professionals in the host country become productive.
HC	P	Migrants provide needed labor.
HC	N	Migrants need expensive services in the host country.
HC	P	Migrants contribute to the host country's prosperity.

Skill Review *Page 145*

CAUSE	EFFECT	TRANSITION WORDS OR PHRASES
differences in culture	misunderstandings between groups	lead to
migration	countries lose most productive workers	as a result of
families are divided	towns lose population	so
immigrants invest skills in new country	few new opportunities in homeland	as a result

Vocabulary Development

Definitions *Page 146*

1. Borders
2. issue
3. homeland
4. typical
5. prosperous
6. Labor
7. allow
8. Income
9. widespread
10. Residents

Word Families *Page 146*

1. wealthy	6. permit
2. original	7. origin
3. migration	8. intend
4. intention	9. migrate
5. wealth	10. permission

Academic Word List *Page 147*

1. residents	6. financial
2. specific	7. migration
3. income	8. labor
4. widespread	9. restrict
5. trends	10. issue

Skills and Strategies 8
Scanning for Specific Information

Skill Practice 1 *Page 150*

1. Beijing	3. Delhi
2. London	4. (over) 25 million

Skill Practice 2 *Page 151*

1. Thomas Malthus: English economist interested in demography
2. 1798
3. Malthusians: People who agree with his ideas
4. war, disease, and smaller families

Reading 3
The Growth of Cities

Connecting to the Topic *Page 152*

Answers will vary.

Previewing and Predicting *Page 152*

A, B, F

While You Read

1. 50 percent
2. trade; religion; security; culture
3. b) European and North American cities
4. squatter settlements
5. Cities have developed in different ways around the world but they also share some features.

Reading Skill Development

Main Idea Check *Page 155*

A 2	D 4
B 5	E 3
C 6	F 1

A Closer Look *Page 155*

1. a, d	5. b, e
2. True	6. True
3. b, d	7. b
4. d	

Skill Review *Page 156*

1. 3 percent	4. a sociologist
2. 3.3 billion	5. the wealthy
3. Europe	6. slums

Vocabulary Development

Definitions *Page 157*

1. urban	6. series
2. harbor	7. suburbs
3. Settlements	8. model
4. pattern	9. Services
5. sociologist	10. critical

Synonyms *Page 157*

1. internal	5. surrounded
2. communities	6. evolved
3. trade	7. vibrant
4. rural	8. sector

Reading 4
Challenges Facing the World's Cities

Connecting to the Topic *Page 159*

Answers will vary.

Previewing and Predicting *Page 159*

SECTION	TOPIC
III	Traffic problems in major cities
III	Breathing problems for residents of cities with bad air pollution
II	People who cannot afford housing and have to live on the street
IV	Communities that use alternative energy
II	Reasons why crime is high in some cities
I	The largest cities in the past and the future
I	A definition of megacities
IV	Planning for better urban living in the future

While You Read

1. cities with a population of more than 10 million people
2. As a result; leads to; results; so; Therefore
3. crime rate; murder rates
4. Another problem in growing cities is pollution.
5. oil and steel plants; chemical factories; respiratory illnesses; air pollution
6. problems with air pollution and heavy traffic; an explosion of new buildings and the loss of parks and open spaces

Reading Skill Development

Main Idea Check *Page 164*

A 5
B 6
C 9
D 2
E 7

A Closer Look *Page 164*

1. c
2. False
3. c
4. c
5. True
6. c
7. a, c, d, e
8. True

Skill Review *Page 165*

1. Megacities; 2020: 35
2. living in poverty; World Bank: 3 billion
3. 60 percent; victims of crime: 2007 United Nations study
4. Jakarta; motorcycle: over 3 million
5. Tianjin-Eco-City: smart growth; wind + solar energy; recycled rain water; 90 percent of transport is public; easy to walk around

Vocabulary Development

Definitions *Page 166*

1. Consequences
2. Nutrition
3. cycle
4. persist
5. generation
6. unique
7. cemetery
8. Tombs
9. bury
10. Respiratory

Words in Context *Page 166*

1. a poverty
   b inequality
   c similar
   d provide
2. e face
   f rate
   g victims
   h huge

Academic Word List *Page 167*

1. sector
2. similar
3. consequences
4. community
5. cycle
6. evolved
7. internal
8. unique
9. persist
10. series

Making Connections

Exercise 1 *Page 169*

2. All countries have experienced some changes in their population growth. This growth has occurred at different times in different parts of the world. Europe and North America had an explosion in population growth in the early nineteenth century. In contrast, many African and Latin American countries began to grow rapidly in the twentieth century.

3. Better hygiene and healthcare have increased life expectancy in many countries. A simple change, the introduction of soap in the nineteenth century, made a big difference in life expectancy. Medicines that prevent disease have made an even bigger difference. However, there are still some countries today where the life expectancy is low because of the low standard of hygiene and healthcare.

4. How do we know the population of different countries? Some countries like Canada and England count their inhabitants every 10 years. In contrast, France counts every seven years, and Japan and Australia count their inhabitants every five years. This information provides an estimate of the worldwide population.

Exercise 2 *Page 170*

1. CAB
2. ACB
3. CAB
4. CBA
5. CBA

5 Design in Everyday Life

Skills and Strategies 9
Vocabulary Study

Skill Practice 1 *Page 173*

Answers will vary. Cards should look like the examples on page 173.

Skill Practice 2 *Page 174*

Answers will vary. Cards should look like the examples on page 173.

Skill Practice 3 *Page 174*

Answers will vary. Cards should look like the examples on page 173.

Reading 1
The Design of Everyday Objects

Connecting to the Topic *Page 175*

Answers will vary.

Previewing and Predicting *Page 175*

A, B, D, E

While You Read

1. only craftsmen could make beautiful objects; now machines could mass-produce at a low cost
2. design principle
3. main idea: many products fail the basic test of usability. However, a few simple changes could improve their usability.
   examples:
   - a long horizontal bar across a door tells users to push
   - A short vertical handle on one side of the door tells users to pull
   - an oven is turned on, a light should show that the oven is on.
   - If batteries must go in one direction, the product design should make it impossible to put them in the other direction.
4. they may not like it because it is too complicated
5. negative impact

Reading Skill Development

Main Idea Check *Page 179*

A 4	D 3
B 8	E 6
C 5	

A Closer Look *Page 179*

1. d	5. True
2. False	6. a
3. b, e	7. c
4. a	

Skill Review *Page 180*

Answers will vary.

Vocabulary Development

Definitions *Page 181*

1. carve	6. conflict with
2. complex	7. visual
3. basic	8. persuade
4. Principles	9. Pleasure
5. store	10. luxury

Words in Context *Page 181*

1. leather	5. confusing
2. decorated	6. owner
3. symbols	7. pay attention to
4. prefer	8. identity

Reading 2
Ergonomics

Connecting to the Topic *Page 183*

Answers will vary.

Previewing and Predicting *Page 183*

A

	FIGURE 5.1	PHOTO
Feet flat on the floor	✓	
Back straight	✓	
Keyboard flat	✓	
Support for arms	✓	
Support for back	✓	
Wrists straight	✓	
Monitor at eye level	✓	

B

b

While You Read

1. efficiency; human comfort
2. a desk, chair, and computer
3. your elbows at an open angle
   Your feet should be flat on the ground.
   The chair back should not be straight, however.
   wrists relaxed and straight.
4. laptop computers are increasing the chance of
   workplace injury

Reading Skill Development

Main Idea Check *Page 186*

A 4   D 2
B 3   E 6
C 7

A Closer Look *Page 186*

1. b   4. d
2. c, d   5. c
3. a, d

Skill Review *Page 187*

Paragraph 6:
Main idea: *Laptops are especially likely to cause injury.*
  Supporting detail: *More people are using laptops as their main computer*
  Supporting detail: *Laptops are not ergonomically designed*
  Supporting detail: *Use of laptops by children is increasing.*

Paragraph 7:
Main idea: *Ergonomic design has economic benefits.*
  Supporting detail: *Treatment for injuries caused by poor design costs a lot of money*
  Supporting detail: *People miss work because of injuries, which is also expensive for businesses.*

Vocabulary Development

Definitions *Page 188*

1. Equipment   6. Posture
2. device   7. involve
3. Strain   8. Height
4. Joints   9. lean
5. Muscles   10. miss

Word Families *Page 188*

1. injured   6. selection
2. adjustable   7. risked
3. risky   8. relaxation
4. injuries   9. selected
5. adjust   10. relax

Academic Word List *Page 189*

1. relax   6. conflicts with
2. injured   7. identity
3. symbol   8. principles
4. complex   9. visual
5. devices   10. involves

Skills and Strategies 10
Taking Notes from a Reading

Skill Practice 1 *Page 192*

Answers will vary.

  Before the invention of the sewing machine, clothes were made by hand one at a time. This took a long time. (Technology, however, has completely changed the manufacturing of clothes.) *1* In the 1830s, the sewing machine was invented. This changed the way clothes were made. Military uniforms were the first items of clothing to be produced using this technology. Production increased as technology continued to change. *2* In 1859, a foot pedal was added to the sewing machine. Now clothing could be made more quickly. *3* Later, after the invention of the electric sewing machine, clothing could easily be mass-produced. *4* More recently, computer technology has dramatically changed the design and manufacture of clothes. It now takes only 90 minutes for computers and automatic machines to make a man's suit. This is a huge savings in time and labor from the hard, slow work of sewing by hand.

Skill Practice 2 *Page 192*

Answers will vary.
I. Skirts – long history
  A. Ancient times
    1. Men and women wore skirts
    2. *Skirts made of animal fur*
  B. *18th century*
    1. *Men did not wear skirts*
    2. Women's skirts were long + full. 2 meters across
  C. *1920s*
    1. *Skirts raised to the knees*
  D. Modern times
    1. *1960s – miniskirts*
    2. Late 1970s, miniskirts were no longer popular.

Skill Practice 3 *Page 193*

Answers will vary.

    An interior designer is a person who designs the spaces where people work and live. The demand for interior designers is growing in the United States; however, students should think carefully before choosing this career. They need to understand what skills they must have. *1* First, an interior designer needs to have advanced computer skills because many companies use software programs for design. *2* Second, they need to understand the basics of engineering and art. *3* Good communication skills are also very important. Designers must clearly explain their ideas to their customers. *4* Finally, designers usually need a college degree. After they receive the degree, they will need to work for about three years at a beginning level. During this time, the salary is not very high. Students should also know that the number of interior designers is expected to grow. *5* As a result, it will soon be quite difficult to find design work because so many people are choosing interior design as a career.

I. *Interior design – think before choosing career*
  A. *Skills needed*
    1. *Computer skills*
    2. *Engineering and art*
    3. *Communication skills*
    4. *College degree*
  B. *After college*
    1. *3 years at beginning level*
    2. *low salary*
  C. *Number of designers increasing*
    1. *difficult to find a job*

Reading 3
The Design of Living Space

Connecting to the Topic *Page 194*

Answers will vary.

Previewing and Predicting *Page 194*

A, B, D

While You Read

1. c) peaceful
2. whereas; active
3. the head of the bed should point in the correct direction; bedroom should not have any mirrors in it because mirrors make it difficult to remove negative energy.
4. red is the most exciting and stimulating color; green is a more peaceful color; Blue; peace and stability; White; a color of balance.
5. Traditional designers think of horizontal, or floor space. In contrast, designers of small living spaces say that they try to use three-dimensional space.

Reading Skill Development

Main Idea Check *Page 197*

A 5   D 4
B 3   E 2
C 1

A Closer Look *Page 197*

1. c   5. a
2. False   6. a, b, d
3. b, c, e   7. c
4. 1b; 2d; 3c; 4a

Skill Review *Page 198*

Answers will vary.

Vocabulary Development

Definitions *Page 199*

1. reflect
2. stranger
3. organized
4. combination
5. Passion
6. stimulating
7. represent
8. masculine
9. dresser
10. three-dimensional

Words in Context *Page 199*

1. a personalities
   b calm
   c styles
   d stability

2. e guidelines
   f interior
   g achieve
   h balance

Reading 4
Fashion

Connecting to the Topic *Page 201*

Answers will vary.

Previewing and Predicting *Page 201*

SECTION	HEADING	TOPICS	✓
II	Fashion and Identity	A history of fashion	✓
		Fashion and self-expression	✓
		How clothes are made	
		Changes in women's fashions	✓
		Top designers in women's fashions	
III	How Fashion Moves through Society	Factors in fashion trends	✓
		Tattoos as fashion	✓
		Where to study about fashion	
		The role of designers in fashion trends	✓
		Fashion trends in Asia	
IV	Why Fashions Change	What is coming next in fashion	✓
		How young people affect fashion	✓
		The business of fashion	✓
		The science of fashion	
		How to start a clothing business	

While You Read

1. where they were from, their job, their class, and sometimes even their religion
2. The history of women's clothing is another good example of the powerful messages that clothing can send.
3. The fashions that began as very expensive designs eventually appear in shopping malls.
4. Hip-hop design is a good example of street fashion
5. *Possible answers*: street styles; fashion trends; hip-hop artists; clothing sales; sports shoes; clothing companies; shoe companies
6. Young people play an especially important role in how fashion changes.

Reading Skill Development

Main Idea Check *Page 206*

A 11
B 9
C 4
D 10
E 3

A Closer Look *Page 206*

1. c
2. a, b, d, e
3. b
4. C → D → A → E → B
5. False
6. B → A → D → C

Skill Review *Page 207*

1. Think about the clothes you are wearing right now. Why did you choose to buy these clothes? And why did you choose to wear them today? Like most people, you probably chose them for several reasons. Perhaps you bought them because of their price. Perhaps you are wearing them because they are comfortable. However, it is also likely that there was another important reason for your choices – fashion – the styles that are popular now.

2. Slowly women's fashion began to change. During World War I, *E* women in many countries had to go to work for the first time because *C* men were fighting in the war. Women worked in offices, in factories, and on farms. In order to *C* work safely, they needed a style of clothes that was different from the long, full dresses that were common at that time, *E* so many of them began to wear pants. Many women still choose to wear pants.

Vocabulary Development

Definitions *Page 208*

1. jewelry
2. message
3. class
4. bind
5. aware
6. military
7. adopt
8. Outsiders
9. public
10. heel

Synonyms *Page 208*

1. leisure
2. dominant
3. prison
4. tough
5. appeal
6. survey
7. normal
8. acknowledge

Academic Word List *Page 209*

1. military
2. dominant
3. surveys
4. acknowledged
5. guidelines
6. normal
7. aware
8. achieve
9. stability
10. styles

Making Connections

Exercise 1 *Page 211*

1. Objects are often redesigned in order to improve their usability. One example of this is wheeled luggage. People no longer strain joints and muscles because they don't have to lift heavy luggage. This results in fewer injuries.

2. The Museum of Modern Art in New York has a collection of everyday objects. A paper clip, a bottle opener, and a plastic top on a cup are examples of objects in the museum. These objects all provide simple solutions to everyday problems. Because they are functional and easy to use, these objects have become a part of everyday life.

3. Interior designers work in many different types of spaces. Some focus on one aspect of design, such as preventing repeated injuries with computers. Others, however, design homes and create spaces that reflect the owners' personalities. A third group may design specific spaces, such as hotel rooms.

4. It is important to be comfortable when you are driving for a long time. Before you drive, you should adjust the seat to correspond to your height. You should also adjust your seat to lean backward a little bit. Finally, make sure the safety belt is flat over your shoulder.

5. Musicians have always influenced fashion design. For example, Elvis Presley dominated rock music in the late 1950s and early 1960s. His music and fashion reflected new ideas at that time and were very popular. Because of his popularity, young people adopted his style and wore "Elvis clothes."

Exercise 2 *Page 212*

1. CBA
2. BAC
3. BCA
4. ACB
5. BAC

6 The Brain and Behavior

Skills and Strategies 11
Collocations

Skill Practice 1 *Page 216*

1. pay – to
2. to
3. making
4. plays a – in
5. for

Skill Practice 2 *Page 216*

1. video games
2. develop
3. follow
4. push
5. at
6. a challenge
7. take – of

Skill Practice 3 *Page 217*

Dr. Alan Hirsch thinks he can predict personality from which snack foods a person prefers. Hirsch, a scientist from the Smell and Taste Treatment and Research Foundation, has spent more than 20 years studying this issue. He has asked more than 18,000 Americans about their favorite salty snack. He found that people who like tortilla chips (a Mexican-style snack) want everything to be perfect. If you want someone you can depend on, you need to find someone who prefers peanuts. They are never late for appointments. Hirsch can also predict personalities based on ice-cream flavor preferences. Do you like vanilla? You are probably a private person, but you like to take risks. Are you a chocolate lover? You like to be the center of attention, and you get bored easily. Strawberry? You should avoid stress. People who like strawberries worry about everything!

1. spent – years
2. depend on
3. late for
4. based on
5. take risks
6. avoid stress
7. worry about

Reading 1
Brain Development and Function

Connecting to the Topic *Page 218*

Answers will vary.

Previewing and Predicting *Page 218*

PARAGRAPH	QUESTION
7	Do we know everything about the brain?
3	How has technology helped us to learn about the brain?
5	Does the brain change as we grow?
6	What happens to the brain in old age?
2	What are the parts of the brain?
4	How do humans understand information?

While You Read

1. involved in; play an important role; responsible for
2. or pictures
3. because
4. older people who stay physically and mentally active continue to make and keep neural connections

Reading Skill Development

Main Idea Check *Page 222*

A 5
B 6
C 3
D 2
E 4

A Closer Look *Page 222*

1. 1 c, e; 2 b; 3 f; 4 a, d
2. False
3. a, b
4. False
5. b
6. False

Skill Review *Page 223*

A

1. decisions
2. information
3. a role
4. into
5. for
6. to
7. up
8. in
9. to
10. to

B

1. interested in
2. access to
3. lights up
4. plays; role
5. send information
6. make decisions
7. divided into
8. flows to
9. responsible for
10. connected to

Vocabulary Development

Definitions *Page 224*

1. structure
2. function
3. neurons
4. resemble
5. diagnose
6. patient
7. consistent
8. surge
9. remain
10. treat

Words in Context *Page 224*

1. process
2. indicate
3. back and forth
4. keep track of
5. nervous system
6. involved in
7. Prior to
8. consists of

Reading 2
The Teenage Brain

Connecting to the Topic *Page 226*

Answers will vary.

Previewing and Predicting *Page 226*

Answers will vary.

While You Read

1. the brain is only about 80 percent developed at adolescence
2. There is another surge of growth in neurons in early adolescence. **However**, this growth begins in the back of the brain in areas that control language and vision. The teenagers were using a part of the brain related to emotion. **In contrast**, the adults were using a part of the brain related to judgment and planning.
3. good at; respond to; compared to; related to; angry at
4. Another factor that makes it hard for teenagers to use good judgment is lack of sleep.
6. video chat; check Facebook; text their friends; listen to music; do their homework
7. commit a crime; taking into account; result in

Reading Skill Development

Main Idea Check *Page 230*

A 3   D 6
B 2   E 5
C 4

A Closer Look *Page 230*

1. b, c
2. a, c, d, e
3. b
4. True
5. b
6. d
7. a, d

Skill Review *Page 231*

1. Until recently, scientists believed that dramatic changes in hormones caused this teenage behavior. However, new research suggests that hormones are not the only cause.
2. There is another surge of growth in neurons in early adolescence. However, this growth begins in the back of the brain in areas that control language and vision.
4. As children become adults, it is important for them to become independent, to explore unfamiliar situations, and to have new experiences. Sometimes, however, this leads teenagers to take part in risky behavior.
5. They need 9 hours of sleep every day in order to function well. However, a recent study found that 90 percent of teenagers get less than 9 hours of sleep a night, and that 10 percent get less than 6 hours.
6. Some evidence suggests that multitasking improves some skills. Hand-eye coordination, for example, improves by playing video games. However, scientists have also found that there are negative effects.

Vocabulary Development

Definitions *Page 232*

1. Adolescence
2. adulthood
3. Hormones
4. examine
5. related
6. crucial
7. lack of
8. stay up
9. certain
10. Coordination

Word Families *Page 232*

1. maturity
2. stressful
3. response
4. independence
5. judgment
6. stress
7. independent
8. mature
9. respond
10. judge

Academic Word List *Page 234*

1. stressful
2. adulthood
3. functions
4. process
5. crucial
6. Prior to
7. consists of
8. consistent
9. mature
10. responds

Skills and Strategies 12
Preparing for a Reading Test

Skill Practice 1 *Page 236*

1. A scientist who studies the brain
2. Brain mapping / images of brain activity
3. Frontal lobes

Skill Practice 2 *Page 237*

Possible questions:
1. What are the two halves of the brain called?
2. Which hemisphere is connected to analytical thinking?
3. How would you describe right-brain thinkers?

Skill Practice 3 *Page 237*

Answers will vary.

Reading 3
The Male and Female Brain

Connecting to the Topic *Page 238*

Answers will vary.

Previewing and Predicting *Page 238*

PARAGRAPH	QUESTION
6	What is female intuition?
3	How do differences in the male and female brain change as girls and boys grow older?
4	What are some differences between the adult male brain and the adult female brain?
7	Why did men's and women's brains develop differently?
5	How do male and female brains process information?

While You Read

1. responsible for; divided into; connected by
2. girls remembered people / boys remembered objects; boys – trucks, machines, building blocks / Girls dolls; boys play and fight physically / girls play more quietly.
3. a task requiring spatial ability
4. How did these differences in male and female brains develop? Researchers believe this was connected to human survival.

Reading Skill Development

Main Idea Check *Page 242*

A	2	D	3
B	6	E	7
C	4	F	5

A Closer Look *Page 242*

1. False
2. b, d
3. b, d
4. a
5. b, c, e
6. c
7. True

Skill Review *Page 243*

A
1. The left hemisphere
2. Corpus callosum
3. Men mainly use the left hemisphere; women use both hemispheres.

B
Answers will vary.

Vocabulary Development

Definitions *Page 244*

1. conduct
2. experiment
3. tend to
4. Spatial
5. imagine
6. Intuition
7. sense
8. interpret
9. hunters
10. intelligent

Synonyms *Page 244*

1. recall
2. biology
3. distinct
4. capacity
5. extensive
6. superior
7. collected
8. route

Reading 4
Addiction and the Brain

Connecting to the Topic *Page 246*

Answers will vary.

Previewing and Predicting *Page 246*

A, C, D, E

While You Read

1. send messages from one neuron to another
2. reduce the amount; interrupt this process; keep smoking
3. brain releases dopamine; feeling of pleasure; drugs imitate this process; brain interprets the drug as pleasure
4. at work; shut down; focus on; controls judgment; responds to
5. stress increases the chance that people will become addicts
6. admit they have a problem; stay away from the people and places connected to the addiction; have to stay at special treatment centers

Reading Skill Development

Main Idea Check *Page 250*

A 2
B 9
C 7
D 8
E 5

A Closer Look *Page 250*

1. c, e
2. C → E → A → B → D
3. False
4. a
5. True
6. b
7. b
8. b, d

Skill Review *Page 251*

A
1. A neurotransmitter that sends messages of pleasure
2. Stops the brain from controlling the amount of dopamine
3. Dopamine levels sharply increase.

B
Answers will vary.

Vocabulary Development

Definitions *Page 252*

1. attitude
2. breakthrough
3. Nicotine
4. desire
5. purchase
6. imitate
7. Physically
8. Genetic
9. vaccine
10. Antibodies

Words in Context *Page 252*

A
1. e
2. d
3. f
4. a
5. h
6. c
7. b
8. g

B
Answers will vary.

Academic Word List *Page 253*

1. conduct
2. interpret
3. clarify
4. purchase
5. attitude
6. physically
7. distinct
8. route
9. capacity
10. intelligent

Making Connections

Exercise 1 *Page 255*

1. Some people suffer from loss of memory as they get older. Normally they lose their most recent memories first. Gradually, they forget other things including even where they live. This can cause a lot of stress for the people who love them.

2. There are several distinct types of memory. One type is known as short-term memory. Researchers have conducted experiments to understand more about short-term memory. As a result of these experiments, they have found that short-term memory means that humans can remember things for only about 30 seconds.

3. Humans have very good vision compared to many other animals. Other animals do not have good vision, but their other senses are powerful. For example, cats have an excellent sense of smell and hearing. On the other hand, some insects cannot hear, but they are sensitive to very small movements.

4. An atlas is usually a book of maps, but scientists are working on a new kind of atlas – an atlas of the brain. This atlas consists of images of 7,000 healthy brains. The scientists plan to put these images on the Internet so that people can see them in three dimensions. Scientists hope that these images will lead to greater understanding of the brain.

5.   Several <u>studies</u> have explored the idea that <u>music</u> can improve <u>intelligence</u>. One <u>study</u> claimed that <u>music</u> lessons could <u>improve</u> spatial processing. <u>Another study</u> tried to show that <u>music</u> <u>lessons</u> <u>improve</u> memory. <mark>However</mark>, no <u>studies</u> have been able to show a consistent beneficial effect of <u>music</u> on <u>intelligence</u>.

Exercise 2 *Page 256*

1. BAC
2. CBA
3. CBA
4. ACB
5. CAB

Quizzes

Reading Quiz · Unit 1

Read the passage. Then answer the questions that follow.

Photojournalism: A Dangerous Job

Journalists play an important role in modern society. They make sure that the public   1
has free and open access to information. However, when journalists cover stories in
locations affected by war or natural disasters, their work can be dangerous. This work
is hazardous for all journalists, but for photojournalists – photographers that cover the
news – the job is especially dangerous. Reporters that write their stories can sometimes
cover events from a distance. They can also find out about a story on the telephone or
through Internet communication. Photojournalists, in contrast, must be right where the
action and the danger are.

Technology has changed the way photojournalists work. The first photojournalists   2
appeared in the 1850s and 1860s during the Crimean War and the American Civil
War. They took only still photographs, but during World War I, photojournalists began
taking moving pictures. In those days, the photojournalists' equipment was heavy and
difficult to carry. Today, however, the equipment is very light and portable. This allows
journalists to move quickly and get very close to the action. They can transmit live
videotape of a battle, a fire, or violent storm.

Photographs are very influential and can often have a greater impact than words.   3
They are particularly important today when people often don't have time to read a
whole news story. Instead, they may just scan it quickly and look at the photographs
that accompany the story. As a result of the increasing importance of photographs,
photojournalists are under pressure to get the most impressive images.

Photojournalists accept the risks of their job. It has sometimes been said that   4
every photojournalist wants to find an image that will save a life or stop a war. That
is probably not likely to happen, but there have been powerful photographs that have
dramatically changed public opinion.

Because today's photojournalists can cover their stories so closely, they sometimes   5
find themselves in situations that they cannot control. As a result, many photojournalists
are injured every year. Some of them die, mostly in war zones. In 2011, 34 journalists
were killed while on the job, many of them photojournalists.

There are also psychological risks. When they are photographing a dangerous or   6
dramatic situation, many photojournalists feel a sense of conflict. Should they get the
best picture or do they have a responsibility to help the person they are photographing?
Some photojournalists say that this conflict is more difficult to manage than the physical
danger. In the end, however, they say that if their photographs can change just one
person's mind, then the risks are worthwhile.

Reading Quiz · Unit 1 (continued)

A Main Idea Check

1. What is the main idea of the reading? (5 points)
   a. The job of photojournalists has changed a lot in the last 150 years.
   b. Photojournalism is a dangerous but very important job.
   d. Photojournalists can have a lot of influence on public opinion.

2. Match each paragraph main idea below to a paragraph from the reading. Write the number of the paragraph on the blank line. (5 points)

   _____ Photographs have a major impact in news stories today.

   _____ Photojournalists often face psychological challenges.

   _____ Photojournalism has changed with advances in technology.

B A Closer Look
Look back at the reading to answer the following questions. (2 points each)

1. Photojournalists' work is often more dangerous than writing news stories. **True or False?**

2. Why has photojournalism become more dangerous today than in the past?
   a. It is more dangerous to take modern videos than still photographs.
   b. Photojournalists take greater risks because they want to stop wars.
   c. New technology has allowed them to come closer to dangerous situations.

3. According to the reading, in what situations do most photojournalists die?
   a. In natural disasters   c. In fires
   b. In wars   d. In fights

4. Choose the correct two items below to complete the sentence:
   Photojournalists often have to choose between _____ and _____.
   a. getting a great image   c. avoiding danger
   b. influencing people   d. helping the people they photograph

5. Thirty-four photojournalists were killed in 2011. **True or False?**

C Definitions
Find words in the reading that can complete the following definitions. (2 points each)

1. To _____ a news story is to report on it. (*v*) Par. 1

2. Something that is _____ is dangerous. (*adj*) Par. 1

3. If something is _____, you can take it with you from place to place easily. (*adj*) Par. 2

4. To _____ something is to look at it or read it quickly. (*v*) Par. 3

5. When things or events _____ each other, they go together or happen at the same time. (*v*) Par. 3

Vocabulary Quiz · Unit 1

A The words in the box are words that you studied in Unit 1. Choose the best word to complete each sentence. You will not use all the words. (2 points each)

appetite	available	average	benefit	concept	convenient
documents	ignore	influence	privacy	significant	terrified

1. A smart phone is a very _____ way to get news and other information.

2. The Internet makes it difficult for celebrities to have much _____ in their lives.

3. Newspapers tend to place the most _____ news stories on the front page.

4. In the digital age, many wonder if printed newspapers will still be _____ five years from now.

5. The public's _____ for the latest technology keeps companies like Apple alive.

6. Some residents were _____ listening to reports of the approaching hurricane.

7. The reporter was able to confirm his story with the _____ sent to him by his informant.

8. You can probably _____ most of what you read in the magazines in supermarket checkout lines.

B Circle the letter of the best word to complete each sentence. The answer is always an Academic Word List word from the unit. (2 points each)

1. After the storm, no news could be _____ for several hours until computers came back online.
   a. transmitted   b. rejected   c. accelerated   d. influenced

2. The news reported that there was only one _____ of the plane crash.
   a. immigrant   b. survivor   c. villager   d. addict

3. The editor _____ the writer's story because none of the facts could be checked.
   a. attacked   b. rejected   c. benefitted   d. focused on

4. Social media can have a greater _____ on society than other types of media.
   a. devastation   b. pressure   c. impact   d. pace

5. The private lives of famous people sometimes become _____ to all because of the Internet.
   a. accessible   b. influential   c. worthwhile   d. fake

6. With some interesting artwork, you can _____ a boring webpage into an exciting one.
   a. research   b. reject   c. pretend   d. transform

7. He worked for _____ news media for 20 years before starting an online news source.
   a. traditional   b. eager   c. negative   d. shocked

Skills and Strategies Quiz · Unit 1

A Skills and Strategies 1: Understanding Vocabulary in Context
Answer the following questions about Skills and Strategies 1. (2 points each)

1. When you meet a word you don't know while reading, you should stop reading and quickly look it up in a dictionary. **True or False?**

2. A strategy to use when you don't know the meaning of a word while you are reading is to _____.
   a. look for clues in the same sentence
   b. look for clues in the next sentence
   c. look for clues in the previous sentence
   d. all of the above

3. Choose the correct word or phrase to complete the sentence.
   A definition may be introduced by _____ or _____.
   a. or   b. for example   c. that is   d. whereas

4. Which strategy would you use to guess the meaning of the word in bold?
   *Unlike those who stop believing in their dreams, those who **persist** will succeed.*
   a. definition   b. exemplification   c. contrast   d. general knowledge

5. After the context clue signal *such as* you would probably find an example.
   True or False?

B Skills and Strategies 2: Finding Main Ideas
Answer the following questions about Skills and Strategies 2. (2 points each)

1. The main idea of a paragraph is typically expressed in the first sentence of a paragraph.
   True or False?

2. The topic of a paragraph is _____.
   a. the main idea   c. the writer's opinion
   b. the general subject

3. Not all paragraphs have a main idea. **True or False?**

4. Choose the correct two items to complete the sentence.
   A main idea contains both a/an _____ and a/an _____.
   a. topic   b. example   c. restatement   d. claim

5. Pay attention to the last sentence of longer paragraphs because it _____.
   a. often restates the main idea of the paragraph
   b. usually contains the topic of the paragraph
   c. may tell you about the main idea of the next paragraph

Reading Quiz · Unit 2

Read the passage. Then answer the questions that follow.

El Sistema – Changing Education and Communities

Education is about learning math, science, and history, right? Perhaps, but one man in Venezuela is sure that education is about a lot more than that.   1

Dr. José Abreu sees education as a way out of poverty for children and a way to change communities. He thinks this is all possible through music education. In 1975, Dr. Abreu began El Sistema (Spanish for *The System*), a program that provides an education in classical music to the young people of Venezuela, even those who live in the poorest communities.   2

Dr. Abreu wanted the children to have the opportunity to learn classical music, but he also wanted them to learn about personal responsibility, the importance of hard work, and working effectively in a group. He wanted to include the families and communities in order to provide support for the young musicians. Today, more than 300,000 young people in Venezuela are participating in El Sistema. The program has been so successful that it is now expanding rapidly. Programs based on this approach have been launched in locations all over the world and now reach almost 2 million young people.   3

This success made scholars wonder how broad its impact might be. In other words, they wanted to know if the program has impact beyond the development of the children's musical abilities. Several studies of music education have found that it can have a range of positive effects. One study found that studying music "enhances child development, providing intellectual and emotional benefits that last a lifetime." This effect was particularly strong among children who play a musical instrument.   4

In general, music education is associated with higher academic performance, both in math and in reading. One evaluation found that the program promoted students' cognitive, personal, and social skills, in addition to their musical skills. It improved their memory, attention, and confidence. Students in the El Sistema program did better in school than students who were not in the program. They were also far more likely to stay in school until graduation.   5

One aspect of these research findings is particularly important. In poor countries or in poor areas of a country, there is often not a lot of money for education, particularly for music education. Perhaps the government feels that music education is optional and the children should concentrate on their studies in math, language, and science instead. However, it is exactly these poor children who could get the greatest benefit from a music education program like El Sistema.   6

Reading Quiz · Unit 2 (continued)

A Main Idea Check

1. What is the main idea of the whole reading? (5 points)
   a. Venezuela is leading the world in music education.
   b. It is important to begin music education early to get the most benefit.
   c. Music education has a positive impact beyond music.

2. Match each paragraph main idea below to a paragraph from the reading. Write the number of the paragraph on the blank line. (5 points)

   _____ Research shows that music education helps with other skills.

   _____ El Sistema began in Venezuela and was designed to give poor children an opportunity to learn classical music.

   _____ Music education has been especially helpful for poor children.

B A Closer Look
Look back at the reading to answer the following questions. (2 points each)

1. Which one of the following was *not* among the things Dr. Abreu thought children would learn in El Sistema?
   a. classical music   c. mathematics
   b. responsibility   d. how to work with others

2. El Sistema has helped almost 2 million children in Venezuela. **True or False?**

3. What aspect of music education has been found to have the most positive impact?
   a. playing a musical instrument   c. learning about classical music
   b. being able to read music

4. Choose two items below to complete the sentence.
   Music education can have a positive effect on academic performance by improving _____ and _____.
   a. memory   b. social skills   c. responsibility   d. attention

5. The reading suggests that governments without much money for education should concentrate on math and science first. **True or False?**

C Definitions
Find words in the reading that can complete the following definitions. (2 points each)

1. If something has a/an _____ impact, it affects a lot of people or a lot of things. (*adj*) Par. 4

2. To _____ something is to make it better or stronger. (*v*) Par. 4

3. _____ means related to advanced ideas and thinking. (*adj*) Par. 4

4. _____ skills are related to thinking and learning. (*adj*) Par. 5

5. If something is _____, it is not required. (*adj*) Par. 6

Vocabulary Quiz · Unit 2

A The words in the box are words that you studied in Unit 2. Choose the best word to complete each sentence. You will not use all the words. (2 points each)

collaborate	colony	compete	curiosity	curriculum	efficient
encounter	essential	funding	incorporate	obsolete	shortage

1. Students today often must _____ on group assignments.

2. In the new _____, students must study computer programming.

3. Has technology made learning basic addition and subtraction _____?

4. A student can never have too much _____ about life.

5. The government provides _____ for public education.

6. Katie tried to _____ different types of music into her dance performance.

7. It is _____ to have a good knowledge of English in the twenty-first century.

8. Since there is a/an _____ of qualified teachers, there are many job openings right now.

B Circle the letter of the best word to complete each sentence. The answer is always an Academic Word List word from the unit. (2 points each)

1. It is important for education nowadays to _____ the skills necessary in the global economy.
   a. design   b. criticize   c. emphasize   d. launch

2. School officials _____ that more students will graduate from college this year than ever before.
   a. estimate   b. measure   c. argue   d. obtain

3. _____ show that more women than men graduate from college in the United States.
   a. Scores   b. Arguments   c. Evaluations   d. Statistics

4. The teacher tries to _____ classroom activities so the children won't get bored.
   a. analyze   b. vary   c. compare   d. require

5. Parents _____ their children's education in many ways, sometimes more than teachers.
   a. contribute to   b. approach   c. expand   d. lend

6. Under the new university _____, students who miss a final exam will fail the class.
   a. location   b. shortage   c. evaluation   d. policy

7. Getting high grades in all your classes will _____ a lot of hard work and effort.
   a. estimate   b. require   c. encounter   d. evaluate

Skills and Strategies Quiz · Unit 2

A Skills and Strategies 3: Using the Dictionary

Answer the following questions about Skills and Strategies 3. (2 points each for questions 1–3; 4 points for question 4)

1. The most important time to use a dictionary while you are reading is when you _____.
   a. see a word that you don't know
   b. see a word that you think you know but you're not sure of its meaning
   c. figure out the meaning of a key word from the context
   d. try to use the context to figure out the meaning of a key word but you fail

2. Choose the correct word or phrase to complete the sentence.
   A dictionary entry of a word usually contains its pronunciation, definition, and _____.
   a. part of speech   b. origin   c. frequency of use   d. an example sentence

3. If there is more than one meaning for a word in the dictionary, you should use the first one. **True or False?**

4. Identify four parts of a dictionary entry.

   _____ 1. Definition
   _____ 2. Synonym
   _____ 3. Part of speech
   _____ 4. Example sentence

   a   b   c   d   e   f
   | | | | | |
   pupil <student> /ˈpju·pəl/ *n* a person who is
   being taught, especially a child at school · *There
   are about fifteen pupils in the dance class.*

B Skills and Strategies 4: Finding Supporting Details

Answer the following questions about Skills and Strategies 4. (2 points each for questions 1–3; 4 points for question 4)

1. Supporting statements are necessary to make a writer's main idea _____.
   a. believable   b. interesting   c. true   d. different

2. Sometimes supporting details can be found in the main idea sentence. **True or False?**

3. Which of the following is *not* a transition word or phrase that signals a supporting detail?
   a. In the future   b. such as   c. For this reason   d. Furthermore

4. Identify which is the main idea and which is the supporting detail in the pairs of sentences. Write *MI* on the blank line if it is the main idea and *SD* if it is a supporting detail.

   _____ a. There are many factors that can affect the quality of education that a school provides.

   _____ b. It is clear that class size can make a significant difference in how much students learn.

   _____ c. One change that schools are making is to provide more fresh vegetables and salads.

   _____ d. Many schools are planning new menus to make meals healthier for students.

Name: _____   Date: _____

Reading Quiz · Unit 3

Read the passage. Then answer the questions that follow.

Cell Phones: Help for Small Businesses in the Developing World

Small businesses are vital for a country's economy. They are especially important for developing countries, where they are a significant source of jobs and revenue. Yet small businesses in the developing world face many challenges, such as the following:

- Oudry is a farmer who sells bananas in different villages. He wants to sell them where the demand for bananas is highest, so he can get the best price. However, the roads are very bad, and it takes all day to travel to one village market. He cannot visit all of the local markets, so he must decide where to go before he knows what the price will be.

- Simon repairs bicycles. When he repairs a bicycle, sometimes people don't have money to pay him. They don't use bank or credit cards. Instead, they may say, "My grandfather will pay. He lives in another village." Sometimes it takes a long time for Simon to get his money.

- Anjali is very poor. Her husband does not earn very much money. She wants to earn money to assist him. However, because she has four young children to take care of and she has very little education, it will be difficult for her to find employment.

Is there a solution to these problems? For all of them, the key has been the cell phone. The number of cell phones in the developing world has skyrocketed. There are approximately 6 billion cell phones in the world, and the majority – almost 5 billion – are in the developing world. In India, more people have access to a cell phone than to a modern toilet. Cell phones have become central to the success of businesses in these countries, especially small businesses.

All over the developing world, farmers have increased their incomes by using their cell phones to send and receive information. Farmers like Oudry can find out which village has the best price for his bananas.

In many developing countries, it is difficult for consumers to pay someone who is far away. In Kenya, a company called M-Pesa allows people to pay with their cell phones. Instead of money, they pay with airtime. For example, if Simon repairs a boy's bicycle, the boy's grandfather can pay Simon with airtime even if he lives in a remote village. Simon can use the airtime, or he can pay someone else with it.

In Bangladesh, many women have supplemented their families' income by selling milk or vegetables. In 1997, women like Anjali started selling airtime from their cell phones instead. They borrowed money from a bank to buy the phone, and they paid it back when they earned enough money. These innovations in cell-phone use have helped small businesses grow and have increased prosperity in many developing countries.

Reading Quiz · Unit 3 (continued)

A Main Idea Check

1. What is the main idea of the whole reading? (5 points)
    a. Cell phones are helping women in the developing world to become more independent.
    b. Cell phones are playing a major role in small businesses in the developing world.
    c. Cell phone use is growing faster in the developing world than in the developed world.

2. Match each paragraph main idea below to a paragraph from the reading. Write the number of the paragraph on the blank line. (5 points)

    _____ Cell phones can help owners of different small businesses increase their income.

    _____ Cell phone use in the developing world is growing quickly.

    _____ Cell phone airtime can be used instead of money.

B A Closer Look
Look back at the reading to answer the following questions. (2 points each)

1. How can a cell phone help Oudry?
    a. He can get information about the weather.
    b. He can get information about prices.
    c. He can send out information about his bananas.

2. How can a cell phone help Simon?
    a. He can get paid more quickly.
    b. He can tell customers about his business.
    c. He can get information about bicycles.

3. There are 6 billion cell phones in the developing world. **True or False?**

4. Choose two items below to complete the sentence.
    Cell phone _____ can be used instead of _____.
    a. information   b. airtime   c. milk   d. money

5. Bangladeshi women borrowed money from banks to buy cell phones. They paid the banks back by selling them airtime. **True or False?**

C Definitions
Find words in the reading that can complete the following definitions. (2 points each)

1. If something is _____, it is extremely important. (*adj*) Par. 1

2. _____ is the money that people and businesses pay the government in taxes. (*n*) Par. 1

3. To _____ is to help. (*v*) Par. 1

4. A/An _____ place is far away from where most people live. (*adj*) Par. 4

5. To _____ something is to add to it. (*v*) Par. 5

Vocabulary Quiz · Unit 3

A The words in the box are words that you studied in Unit 3. Choose the best word to complete each sentence. You will not use all the words. (2 points each)

create	crop	drought	emit	employ	event
manufacturing	promote	run out of	share	specialist	surplus

1. The new car factory will _____ 6,500 jobs for the town.

2. He first went to his family doctor, who then sent him to see a heart _____.

3. The tomato _____ froze in last week's cold weather, so prices will be higher next spring.

4. The state has had no rain in more than four months, and officials are now calling this a _____.

5. There are some scientists who predict that we will soon _____ the Earth's supply of petroleum.

6. The company does its sales and marketing in New York, but all of its _____ is done in Asia.

7. Companies worldwide still _____ far more men than women in management positions.

8. In an effort to _____ healthy eating, the employee cafeteria will now sell fresh salads and fruit.

B Circle the letter of the best word to complete each sentence. The answer is always an Academic Word List word from the unit. (2 points each)

1. It was a/an _____ for the company to make a profit during its first year, but sales doubled by its second year.
   a. key   b. team   c. challenge   d. resource

2. The company is expecting the _____ of everyone at the media event.
   a. participation   b. blame   c. effect   d. consumption

3. After the disaster, the Red Cross arrived to _____ food and clothing to survivors.
   a. attract   b. distribute   c. use up   d. hire

4. Everyone must play a _____ in saving our planet, Earth.
   a. consumer   b. ingredient   c. role   d. resource

5. Engineers and scientists continue in their _____ search for new sources of energy.
   a. renewable   b. tropical   c. major   d. constant

6. The city put signs in parks and subways to _____ recycling.
   a. promote   b. attract   c. share   d. emit

7. The advertisements for the sports drink needed to show a fresh and youthful _____.
   a. level   b. image   c. innovation   d. surplus

Skills and Strategies Quiz · Unit 3

A Skills and Strategies 5: The Vocabulary of Numbers

Answer the following questions about Skills and Strategies 5. (2 points each for questions 1–3; 4 points for question 4)

1. The adverb *significantly* shows a small change. **True or False?**

2. Choose the correct word to complete the sentence

   Car sales _____ from 1,200 to 3,600 per month.

   a. doubled   b. tripled   c. fell

3. You should learn the vocabulary of numbers in groups of words that have similar meanings. **True or False?**

4. Match each phrase to a phrase with the same meaning.

   1. increased dramatically   a. went up little by little
   2. declined slightly   b. went up a lot
   3. grew steadily   c. went down a little bit
   4. dropped sharply   d. went down a lot

B Skills and Strategies 6: Information in Graphs and Charts

Answer the following questions about Skills and Strategies 6. (2 points each for questions 1–3; 4 points for question 4)

1. A good reading strategy is to wait until you finish reading a text before studying any graphic information in it. **True or False?**

2. Identify the horizontal axis in this graphic material.

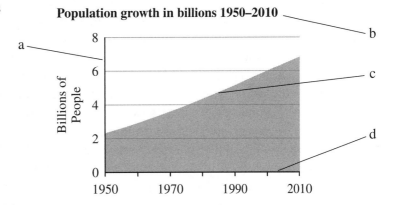

Population growth in billions 1950–2010

3. You should take notes on the information in any graphic material in a reading as well as information in the reading itself. **True or False?**

4. Match the names for different types of graphic material to the figures. Write the letters of the figures on the blank lines.

   _____ 1. A table
   _____ 2. A line graph
   _____ 3. A bar graph
   _____ 4. A pie chart

a
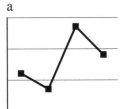

b
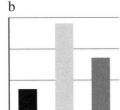

c
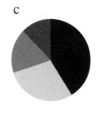

d

Reading Quiz · Unit 4

Read the passage. Then answer the questions that follow.

The World's Population in 2050

There has been huge growth in the world's population over the last 100 years. In 1930, there were 2 billion people on the planet. In 2011, the figure passed 7 billion. According to the United Nations, our population will increase to between 8 billion and 10.5 billion by 2050. The rate of increase has slowed, however. Between 1950 and 2000, the growth rate was 1.76 percent. Between 2000 and 2050, it is predicted to drop to 0.77 percent. Nevertheless, with 1.8 billion women currently of childbearing age, the growth is likely to continue for some time. Demography experts predict that we will reach a stable rate, that is, a rate at which the current population replaces itself, in about 2030.

1

Population trends vary tremendously from one region to another. Population growth increases as a result of increases in three rates: fertility, life expectancy, and immigration. Between now and 2050, the greatest growth is expected in the developing world, particularly in Eastern and Western Africa, where fertility rates remain high. For example, it is predicted that Nigeria will go from 160 million to over 400 million. In Ethiopia, an increase from 91 million to about 278 million is predicted.

2

In contrast, the population in Western Europe and especially Eastern Europe will either grow very slowly or in some cases decline. Compare the examples of Spain and Tanzania. The size of their populations is similar; both have a current population between 46 and 48 million. In 2050, Spain's population will be about the same as it was in 2010, whereas Tanzania's population is expected to triple.

3

Although Spain's population is predicted to remain about the same, some countries in Europe are experiencing a population decrease. This occurs as a result of several factors: a fall in fertility or life expectancy, or significant migration out of the country. In most Eastern European countries, fertility rates have fallen below the replacement rate. In addition, life expectancy is lower in Eastern Europe than in many other parts of the developed world. This is especially true in Russia. Finally, in several Eastern European countries, many people have left for Western Europe or North America.

4

Among wealthy countries, the United States is somewhat unusual. It is expected to continue to grow for two reasons. It has a high immigration rate, and, compared to other countries, it has a fairly high fertility rate. Each population trend creates its own benefits and challenges. Individual governments and international organizations, such as the United Nations, take these issues seriously and will need to develop policies to manage them in the future.

5

Reading Quiz · Unit 4 (continued)

A Main Idea Check

1. What is the main idea of the whole reading? (5 points)

   a. The world's population will look somewhat different in 2050 than it does today.
   b. The world's population will be much larger in 2050 than it is today.
   c. The greatest population growth will be in the developing world.

2. Match each paragraph main idea below to a paragraph from the reading. Write the number of the paragraph on the blank line. (5 points)

   _____ The most rapid population growth will be in the developing world.

   _____ In some parts of Eastern Europe, the population is decreasing.

   _____ The global population will continue to grow but more slowly than in the past.

B A Closer Look
Look back at the reading to answer the following questions. (2 points each)

1. The population will stabilize in 2030. **True or False?**

2. What factor is *not* among the significant factors in population growth?

   a. immigration   c. fertility rates
   b. life expectancy   d. health care

3. The population of Tanzania is likely to be three times larger in 2050. **True or False?**

4. Choose two items below to complete the sentence:

   A drop in the _____ and a rise in _____ has contributed to the population decrease in Eastern European countries.

   a. fertility rate   c. childbearing age
   b. income   d. immigration

5. Why does the U.S. population have a higher rate of increase than other developed countries?

   a. It has a high life expectancy rate.
   b. It is wealthier than other countries.
   c. It has a high immigration rate.

C Definitions
Find words in the reading that can complete the following definitions. (2 points each)

1. _____ is related to the process of having children. (*adj*) Par. 1

2. _____ means to a very great degree. (*adv*) Par. 2

3. To _____ is to go down, to decrease. (*v*) Par. 3

4. To _____ is to become three times larger. (*v*) Par. 3

5. _____ means more than a little but not a lot. (*adv*) Par. 5

Vocabulary Quiz · Unit 4

A The words in the box are words that you studied in Unit 4. Choose the best word to complete each sentence. You will not use all the words. (2 points each)

border	internal	origin	permitted	provide	replaced
series	similar	traded	trend	urban	vibrant

1. Years ago, people traveled to markets in the cities where they _____ food and other goods.

2. In industrialized countries, the _____ has been toward fewer births per woman.

3. The city center is an exciting and _____ area with shopping, restaurants, and street performers.

4. It was impossible for the government to _____ its people with enough food and clean water.

5. Living in a/an _____ area is usually much more expensive than living outside a city.

6. Many of the traditional customs of immigrants are _____ with customs of the new country.

7. You must show your passport every time you cross a country's _____.

8. The _____ conflicts in the country are making it difficult for people to feel safe in their villages.

B Circle the letter of the best word to complete each sentence. The answer is always an Academic Word List word from the unit. (2 points each)

1. The effects of HIV/AIDS are _____ throughout Africa.
   a. specific   b. typical   c. widespread   d. wealthy

2. In Europe, the _____ of workers from the countryside to cities began in the nineteenth century.
   a. migration   b. wealth   c. labor   d. demography

3. The difference in _____ between men and women has decreased over the last 30 years.
   a. support   b. income   c. labor   d. rate

4. Many people of my grandmother's _____ are not comfortable with technology.
   a. generation   b. inequality   c. community   d. pattern

5. It is impossible to imagine the _____ of overpopulation in the poorest areas of the world.
   a. victims   b. residents   c. figures   d. consequences

6. Solutions will slowly _____ to meet the challenges of worldwide population changes.
   a. originate   b. persist   c. evolve   d. allow

7. The U.S. government _____ the number of immigrants who can enter the country each year.
   a. allows   b. restricts   c. permits   d. faces

Skills and Strategies Quiz · Unit 4

A Skills and Strategies 7: Collocations

Answer the following questions about Skills and Strategies 7. (2 points each for questions 1–3; 4 points for question 4)

1. Being aware of collocations helps you read faster because you see groups of words instead of individual words. **True or False?**

2. The phrase *a big crime* is _____.
   a. grammatically incorrect
   b. grammatically correct but not natural
   c. a noun + noun combination
   d. not natural or grammatically correct

3. When a collocation is a noun + noun combination, the second noun acts as an adjective. **True or False?**

4. Match a word from the column on the left to a word from the column on the right to form the most natural collocations.
   _____ 1. powerful   a. economy
   _____ 2. global   b. support
   _____ 3. strong   c. news
   _____ 4. world   d. influence

B Skills and Strategies 8: Scanning for Specific Information

Answer the following questions about Skills and Strategies 8. (2 points each)

1. Scanning is a reading technique that involves reading through a whole text from beginning to end very quickly. **True or False?**

2. Which of the following would you *not* scan for?
   a. a number
   b. the name of an important person in a reading
   c. a date
   d. the main idea of the reading

3. When scanning for specific information, you should *not* _____.
   a. say the words to yourself
   b. move your eyes quickly
   c. slow down when you find the information you are looking for
   d. keep your eyes on the page all the time

4. If you were scanning a text to read about why women in South Korea are getting married later today and having fewer babies than 20 years ago, which of the following would you scan for?
   a. South Korea   c. a year in the 1990s
   b. the word *marriage*   d. all of the above

5. When scanning, focus on the left side of each line of the reading, and move your eyes down the page, looking quickly from left to right. **True or False?**

Reading Quiz · Unit 5

Read the passage. Then answer the questions that follow.

Nature's Design Secrets

Scientists and engineers around the world are studying the design principles of   1
the natural world. They want to use these designs to make new products. The most
prominent product based on nature is Velcro. Velcro is a material that is used in shoes
and clothing. It attaches one piece of material to another. The material was invented by a
Swiss chemist in the middle of the twentieth century. He noticed that after he went for a
walk in the woods, small seeds stuck to his clothing and his dog's fur. He looked at these
seeds under a microscope and discovered that they were covered with very small hooks.
These tiny hooks stuck to everything. He used this idea to create Velcro, a material
covered with hundreds of tiny hooks, just like the seeds.

Unlocking the secret of nature's design is a challenge. It involves paying attention   2
to the smallest details in plants and animals. For example, scientists wondered why a
shark's skin is always so clean. Other fish have bacteria on their skin. They found that
the surface of a shark's skin has a complex pattern that prevents bacteria from sticking.
The scientists are using the sharkskin design to develop a new product. They want
to make a material to cover the interior walls in hospitals. They hope it will prevent
bacteria from spreading and making people sick.

Engineers also use nature's designs. One engineer was working on a project to   3
redesign a high-speed train in Japan. He was aware that the force of air around the train
was slowing it down. He wanted to find a way to reduce this force so that the train could
move faster. He got an idea for a new design from a bird – the kingfisher. The shape
of the kingfisher's head allows it dive into the water without a splash. In other words,
the shape reduces the force of the water. The engineer thought he could use the shape
to reduce the force of air against the train. So, he designed the front of the train in the
shape of the kingfisher's head. This allowed it to move quickly and smoothly, just like a
bird dives into the water.

Scientists and engineers acknowledge that it will be a long time before some of these   4
ideas are used in everyday objects. Nature's designs are incredibly complex, but they
say that the gap between them and human engineering is closing. They have already
achieved success in some areas. These successes have encouraged them to continue
their work.

Reading Quiz · Unit 5 (continued)

A Main Idea Check

1. What is the main idea of the whole reading? (5 points)
   a. Nature's design is very complex and difficult to discover.
   b. Scientists are working on natural designs but so far, they have not been very successful.
   c. Scientists want to use designs from nature to create new products.

2. Match each paragraph main idea below to a paragraph from the reading. Write the number of the paragraph on the blank line. (5 points)

   _____ It may be a while before we see a lot of successful products based on nature.

   _____ Sharkskin may help make hospitals safer.

   _____ Velcro was the first successful product based on design found in nature.

B A Closer Look
Look back at the reading to answer the following questions. (2 points each)

1. The design for Velcro is based on dog's fur. **True or False?**

2. Why is sharkskin special?
   a. It resists bacteria.   c. It is very clean.
   b. It is very complex.

3. What about the kingfisher gave the engineer the idea for his train design?
   a. its feathers   c. the shape of its head
   b. the way that it flies

4. Choose two items below to complete the sentence:
   The train designer compared the force of _____ and _____.
   a. diving   b. surface   c. water   d. air

5. Engineers have already created a lot of products using designs from nature.
   True or False?

C Definitions
Find words in the reading that can complete the following definitions. (2 points each)

1. Something _____ is important and widely known. (*adj*) Par. 1

2. To _____ something means to fasten or connect it to something else.
   (*v*) Par. 1

3. _____ is animal hair. (*n*) Par. 1

4. _____ means very, very small. (*adj*) Par. 1

5. A/An _____ is a space between two things. (*n*) Par. 4

Vocabulary Quiz · Unit 5

A The words in the box are words that you studied in Unit 5. Choose the best word to complete each sentence. You will not use all the words. (2 points each)

adjustable	combination	confusing	guidelines	identify	injured
organized	relax	stimulating	strain	stranger	style

1. A cold shower can be _____ after doing exercise or running.

2. The design of one's home can say a lot about a person's _____.

3. The architect used a/an _____ of stone, glass, and steel, for the building's entrance.

4. The living room is the perfect place to sit back and _____.

5. The seat belt is _____, so you can make it longer or shorter.

6. The instructions for this desk are very _____; I don't know how to begin putting it together.

7. It is much easier to work in a/an _____ space than one where you can't find anything.

8. I've never met that man before; he is a complete _____.

B Circle the letter of the best word to complete each sentence. The answer is always an Academic Word List word from the unit. (2 points each)

1. For some fashion designers, their main _____ of design is comfort.
   a. principle   b. balance   c. interior   d. posture

2. An ergonomically designed office chair will help prevent _____.
   a. stability   b. risk   c. adjustment   d. injury

3. In a/an _____ of 3,000 college students, 78 percent said they often used their laptops while lying in bed.
   a. symbol   b. survey   c. message   d. appeal

4. When receiving the award, the student _____ the help he had received from his professor.
   a. missed   b. reflected   c. persuaded   d. acknowledged

5. All the office workers were involved in _____ the new furniture.
   a. representing   b. conflicting   c. selecting   d. achieving

6. A/an _____ feature of the home is its feng shui design throughout the house.
   a. visual   b. normal   c. dominant   d. luxury

7. When sitting at your office desk, try to be _____ how you sit, place your hands, and hold your mouse.
   a. related to   b. aware of   c. selected for   d. preferred by

Skills and Strategies Quiz · Unit 5

A Skills and Strategies 9: Vocabulary Study
Answer the following questions about Skills and Strategies 9. (2 points each)

1. When you come across an unknown word that is important in the reading and seems useful to know, you should _____.
   a. stop, try to work out its probable meaning, and then continue reading before studying it later
   b. keep reading, then go back to it after you have finished reading, and look it up in a dictionary
   c. stop, write it down on a vocabulary card with its context in the reading, and then study it later

2. You should try to learn all the new words in a reading. **True or False?**

3. Which word in the following sentence would be the least useful to look up in a dictionary?
   The entrance to the gallery is illuminated with incandescent lighting for a softer effect.
   a. entrance   b. gallery   c. illuminated   d. incandescent

4. How should you write a vocabulary notecard?
   a. Side 1: word and definition; Side 2: example sentence
   b. Side 1: word and example sentence; Side 2: definition
   c. Side 1: word only; Side 2 definition and example sentence

5. After you study your vocabulary cards, you should wait a few days before you study them again. **True or False?**

B Skills and Strategies 10: Taking Notes from a Reading
Answer the following questions about Skills and Strategies 10. (2 points each)

1. *Annotating* refers to taking notes in a separate notebook. **True or False?**

2. Choose the phrase that best completes the following sentence.
   An effective outline _____.
   a. presents only the main ideas in a reading
   b. records only the details that you need to study for a test
   c. uses a numbering system
   d. clearly separates the important and less important information of a reading

3. Which of the following would you *not* do on the page of your book when annotating?
   a. write an outline   c. write definitions of key words
   b. circle main ideas   d. number supporting points

4. It's possible to make an outline too detailed. **True or False?**

5. What is the main purpose of outlining and annotating?
   a. To improve vocabulary   c. To learn key terms
   b. To remember information   d. To practice logical thinking

Reading Quiz · Unit 6

Read the passage. Then answer the questions that follow.

Brain Injuries and Sports

Playing sports can be rough, both for professionals and young athletes. There are   1
bumps, collisions, and falls, and sometimes these involve an athlete's head. In some
sports, such as boxing and American football, these blows to the head tend to be an
obvious part of the game, but they occur in other sports as well: team sports like soccer,
hockey, and basketball, and individual sports like skiing, ice skating, and skateboarding.

Regular blows to the head have been an accepted part of these games or sports. Until   2
recently, there was a lack of awareness of their negative impact. A major blow to the
head can lead to a brain injury called a *concussion*. The skull is hard and the brain is
soft. So a strong blow throws the brain against the inside of the skull, which can cause
extensive damage to the neurons in the brain. There is no reliable test for concussions,
so doctors usually diagnose them by observing a patient's behavior. A patient may
become confused and sleepy, have difficulty remembering things, and react slowly. He
or she should not be physically active for a few weeks following a concussion so that the
brain has the chance to recover from the injury. If a patient ignores these symptoms and
does not rest, the impact on behavior and cognitive function could become permanent.

New research suggests that the damage from many small, more minor blows to the   3
head may be just as bad, or even worse than one major blow. The effects of these small
blows can accumulate. What makes this particularly dangerous is that the effects are not
obvious right away. Athletes may not notice that they are injured, so they do not get any
treatment. They just keep playing. When athletes with brain injuries return to the game,
their judgment, coordination, and ability to focus on the game are often impaired. This
makes it more likely that they will be injured a second time. If that injury is a blow to
the head, the damage can be very serious.

Recent research has shown that young athletes are particularly vulnerable to these   4
brain injuries because their brains are not completely mature. In response, experts
recommend that young athletes wear head protection. However, they warn that this can
give athletes a false sense of safety, leading them to take unnecessary risks. Their most
crucial advice is that adults who are involved in athletics for young people should learn
about these injuries. They need to know how to prevent them and how to recognize
their symptoms.

Reading Quiz · Unit 6 (continued)

A Main Idea Check

1. What is the main idea of the whole reading? (5 points)
   a. Concussions are more dangerous for young athletes.
   b. Brain concussions are more dangerous than people once thought.
   c. Concussions are dangerous because many people don't know they have had one.

2. Match each paragraph main idea below to a paragraph from the reading. Write the number of the paragraph on the blank line. (5 points)

   _____ Blows to the head are a regular part of many sports.

   _____ Young brains are the most vulnerable to damage from concussions.

   _____ A concussion from many small blows may be the most dangerous kind.

B A Closer Look
Look back at the reading to answer the following questions. (2 points each)

1. Concussions only occur in team sports. **True or False?**

2. Choose two items below to complete the sentence:
   Common symptoms of a concussion include _____ *and* _____.
   a. confusion   b. bleeding   c. slow reactions   d. pain

3. What should you *not* do after a concussion?
   a. rest for a few days   c. stay active
   b. protect your head

4. Why is a second injury more likely if athletes return to the game after a concussion?
   a. They cannot remember well.   c. They may have a headache.
   b. Their reaction time is slow.

5. Athletes who wear head protection do not have to worry about concussions.
   True or False?

C Definitions
Find words in the reading that can complete the following definitions. (2 points each)

1. A/An _____ occurs when people or things hit each other when they are moving in different directions. (*n*) Par. 1

2. To _____ is to get better after an accident or an illness. (*v*) Par. 2

3. To _____ is to gradually increase or get more of something. (*v*) Par. 3

4. _____ means damaged or less strong. (*adj*) Par. 3

5. Something that is _____ is easily hurt or affected. (*adj*) Par. 4

Vocabulary Quiz · Unit 6

A The words in the box are words that you studied in Unit 6. Choose the best word to complete each sentence. You will not use all the words. (2 points each)

function	imitate	independence	intuition	judgment	keep track of
mature	recall	resemble	spatial	stayed up	surged

1. I know I've met him, but I don't _____ his name.

2. An interior designer must have excellent _____ abilities.

3. The teenage years are when most young people begin to feel the need for more _____.

4. He _____ until 3:00 a.m. so that he could finish the project.

5. The football player was hit hard in the head, but tests showed that his brain _____ was normal.

6. Young people _____ their friends; if their friends smoke, they will, too.

7. Lack of sleep can result in poor _____ and slow reaction time.

8. His family is so large that it's difficult to _____ everyone.

B Circle the letter of the best word to complete each sentence. The answer is always an Academic Word List word from the unit. (2 points each)

1. Doctors had to _____ a series of tests on the patient to determine the cause of his pain.
   a. purchase   b. conduct   c. treat   d. examine

2. She graduated from the university as an intelligent, _____, and kind young woman.
   a. mature   b. superior   c. stressful   d. extensive

3. He asked his boss for more money last week, and he is still waiting for a/an _____.
   a. item   b. attitude   c. chance   d. response

4. Keeping our minds active as we get older is _____ if we want to keep our minds sharp.
   a. distinct   b. stressful   c. crucial   d. genetic

5. There are a lot of data from our research, but now we must _____ them to see what they all mean.
   a. interpret   b. collect   c. diagnose   d. keep track of

6. The button flashes red to _____ that the machine is on.
   a. sense   b. indicate   c. recall   d. imagine

7. Hormones could be one reason why teenagers become _____ in risky activities.
   a. resembled   b. involved   c. judged   d. admitted

Skills and Strategies Quiz · Unit 6

A Skills and Strategies 11: Collocations
Answer the following questions about Skills and Strategies 11. (2 points each)

1. Words that form collocations always appear together; they are never separated.
   True or False?

2. Which of the following does *not* form a collocation?
   a. verb + preposition   c. adjective + verb
   b. verb + noun   d. adjective + preposition

3. Which noun does *not* form a collocation with the verb *to face*?
   a. benefits   b. problems   c. challenges   d. difficulties

4. Some dictionaries list collocations with the word you are looking up. **True or False?**

5. Choose the correct words to complete the sentence.
   He was good _____ math, but he wasn't very interested _____ it.
   a. on   b. in   c. with   d. at

B Skills and Strategies 12: Preparing for a Reading Test
Answer the following questions about Skills and Strategies 12. (2 points each for
questions 1–3, 4 points each for question 4)

1. When you write questions to test yourself, you should only test yourself on the main
   ideas of the reading. **True or False?**

2. Write the following phrases in the correct order on the lines below.
   *predict the questions / when you / is to / an important strategy / study for a test /
   write down the answers / and then to*

   _____

   _____

3. You should put your question cards in a different order each time you study them.
   True or False?

4. Put the steps in preparing for a reading test in the order suggested in Skills and
   Strategies 12.
   _____ a. Think of *wh-* questions
   _____ b. Test yourself
   _____ c. Use notecards to write down your questions and answers
   _____ d. Annotate the reading

Quizzes Answer Key

Unit 1

Reading Quiz – Unit 1

A Main Idea Check
1. b   2. 3, 6, 2

B A Closer Look
1. True   3. b   5. False
2. c   4. a, d

C Definitions
1. cover   4. scan
2. hazardous   5. accompany
3. portable

Vocabulary Quiz – Unit 1

A
1. convenient   5. appetite
2. privacy   6. terrified
3. significant   7. documents
4. available   8. ignore

B
1. a   3. b   5. a   7. a
2. b   4. c   6. d

Skills and Strategies Quiz – Unit 1

A
1. False   3. a, c   5. True
2. d   4. c

B
1. True   3. False   5. a
2. b   4. a, d

Unit 2

Reading Quiz – Unit 2

A Main Idea Check
1. c   2. 5, 2, 6

B A Closer Look
1. c   3. a   5. False
2. False   4. a, d

C Definitions
1. broad   4. Cognitive
2. enhance   5. optional
3. Intellectual

Vocabulary Quiz – Unit 2

A
1. collaborate   5. funding
2. curriculum   6. incorporate
3. obsolete   7. essential
4. curiosity   8. shortage

B
1. c   3. d   5. a   7. b
2. a   4. b   6. d

Skills and Strategies Quiz – Unit 2

A
1. d   3. False
2. a   4. 1. e; 2. b; 3. d; 4. f

B
1. a   3. a
2. False   4. a. MI; b. SD; c. SD; d. MI

Unit 3

Reading Quiz – Unit 3

A Main Idea Check
1. b   2. 1, 2, 4

B A Closer Look
1. b   3. False   5. False
2. a   4. b, d

C Definitions
1. vital   4. remote
2. Revenue   5. supplement
3. assist

Vocabulary Quiz – Unit 3

A
1. create   5. run out of
2. specialist   6. manufacturing
3. crop   7. employ
4. drought   8. promote

B
1. c   3. b   5. d   7. b
2. a   4. c   6. a

Skills and Strategies Quiz – Unit 3

A
1. False
2. tripled
3. True
4. 1. b; 2. c; 3. a; 4. d

B
1. False
2. d
3. True
4. 1. d; 2. a; 3. b; 4. c

Unit 4

Reading Quiz – Unit 4

A Main Idea Check
1. a
2. 2, 4, 1

B A Closer Look
1. True
2. d
3. True
4. a, d
5. c

C Definitions
1. Childbearing
2. Tremendously
3. decline
4. triple
5. Somewhat

Vocabulary Quiz – Unit 4

A
1. traded
2. trend
3. vibrant
4. provide
5. urban
6. replaced
7. border
8. internal

B
1. c
2. a
3. b
4. a
5. d
6. c
7. b

Skills and Strategies Quiz – Unit 4

A
1. True
2. b
3. False
4. 1. d; 2. a; 3. b; 4. c

B
1. False
2. d
3. a
4. d
5. False

Unit 5

Reading Quiz – Unit 5

A Main Idea Check
1. c
2. 4, 2, 1

B A Closer Look
1. False
2. a
3. c
4. c, d
5. False

C Definitions
1. prominent
2. attach
3. Fur
4. Tiny
5. gap

Vocabulary Quiz – Unit 5

A
1. stimulating
2. identity
3. combination
4. relax
5. adjustable
6. confusing
7. organized
8. stranger

B
1. a
2. d
3. b
4. d
5. c
6. c
7. b

Skills and Strategies Quiz – Unit 5

A
1. c
2. False
3. d
4. b
5. False

B
1. False
2. d
3. a
4. True
5. b

Unit 6

Reading Quiz – Unit 6

A Main Idea Check
1. b
2. 1, 4, 3

B A Closer Look
1. False
2. a, c
3. c
4. b
5. False

C Definitions
1. collision
2. recover
3. accumulate
4. Impaired
5. vulnerable

Vocabulary Quiz – Unit 6

A
1. recall
2. spatial
3. independence
4. stayed up
5. function
6. imitate
7. judgment
8. keep track of

B
1. b
2. a
3. d
4. c
5. a
6. b
7. b

Skills and Strategies Quiz – Unit 6

A
1. False
2. d
3. a
4. True
5. d, b

B
1. False
2. When you study for a test, an important strategy is to predict the questions and then to write down the answers.
3. True
4. 1. d; 2. a; 3. c; 4. b